Stafford Library
Columbia College
1001 Rogers Street
Columbia, Missouri 65216

THE NEW ARAB MEDIA

THE NEW ARAB MEDIA

*Technology,
Image and Perception*

EDITED BY
MAHJOOB ZWEIRI AND EMMA C. MURPHY

THE NEW ARAB MEDIA
Technology, Image and Perception

Published by
Ithaca Press
8 Southern Court
South Street
Reading
RG1 4QS
UK

www.ithacapress.co.uk

Ithaca Press is an imprint of Garnet Publishing Limited.

Copyright © Mahjoob Zweiri and Emma C. Murphy, 2011

All rights reserved.
No part of this book may be reproduced in any form or by any electronic or mechanical means, including information storage and retrieval systems, without permission in writing from the publisher, except by a reviewer who may quote brief passages in a review.

First Edition

ISBN-13: 978-0-86372-347-6

British Library Cataloguing-in-Publication Data
A catalogue record for this book is available from the British Library

Typeset by Samantha Barden
Jacket design by Garnet Publishing

Printed in Great Britain by the MPG Books Group,
Bodmin and King's Lynn

Contents

List of Tables and Figures   vii
Contributors   ix

Introduction   xiii
Mahjoob Zweiri and Emma C. Murphy

1   The New Frontier in International Politics: 1
The Nature of al-Jazeera's Prime-time Broadcasting
in Arabic and English
Ahmet Uysal

2   Between Freedom and Coercion: Inside Internet   19
Implantation in the Middle East
Jon W. Anderson

3   The Milestone Metaphor: CNN and al-Jazeera   31
Discourse on the Iraq War
Andreas Musolff and Abdel-mutaleb al-Zuweiri

4   News Media, Public Diplomacy and the 'War on Terror'   47
Saima Saeed

5   Image Culture, Media and Power   69
Khalid Hajji

6   Religious Diaspora and Information Communications   81
Technology: The Impact of Globalization on
Communal Relations in Egypt
Fiona McCallum

7	Between Image and Reality: New ICTs and the Arab Public Sphere *Emma C. Murphy*	103
8	The Impact of Arab Satellite Channels on Public Opinion *Fares Braizat and David Berger*	123
9	Jordan's Local Radio Revolution: Progress, Challenges and Possibilities *Mahjoob Zweiri*	139

Appendix	155
Further Reading	159
Index	163

Tables and Figures

Tables

1.1	News topics on al-Jazeera	7
1.2	Level of news coverage	8
1.3	Area of coverage	9
1.4	News topics by broadcasting/publishing language	10
1.5	Level of coverage in Arabic and English language	11
1.6	Area of coverage in Arabic and English	11
2.1	Comparison of Internet development in Muslim (cultural) and Middle Eastern (political) space, with technological evolution from MIS-based to PC-based to web-based and sociological transitions from Creole Journeys through Elite Contention to today's Postmodern Nomadism	22
3.1	Going public with war	61
3.2	Propaganda and radio	61
8.1	Sample sizes for surveys used in this chapter	124
8.2	Most trusted sources for 'local news'	127
8.3	Most trusted sources for 'Arab regional news'	128
8.4	Most trusted sources for 'international news'	128

Figures

3.1	Media as instruments of war	49
8.1	Percentage of households owning a satellite device	127
8.2	Computer and Internet penetration in Jordan: the percentage of adult Jordanians (18+) who use computers and the Internet	129
8.3	Sources of local news for Jordanians	130
8.4	Sources of Arab news for Jordanians	131
8.5	Sources of international news for Jordanians	132
8.6	Sources of news for Jordanian elites regarding American presidential elections of 2008	135

Contributors

Jon W. Anderson is Professor and Chair of Anthropology at the Catholic University of America and founding editor of *Working Papers on New Media & Information Technology in the Middle East* at Georgetown University's Center for Contemporary Arab Studies, where he is co-director of its Arab Information Project and creator of the first course in the US on new media and information technology in the Arab world. He has, for the past decade, done field research on IT implementation in Egypt, Syria, Jordan, Saudi Arabia and Gulf countries. He has chaired committees on electronic communication for the Middle East Studies Association and the American Anthropological Association; has served on the Social Science Research Council Committee on Information Technology, International Development and Global Security; and is author of *Vers une théorie techno-pratique de l'Internet dans le monde Arab* (Maghreb-Machrek, 2004), 'New Media, New Publics: Reconfiguring the Public Sphere of Islam', *Social Research* (2003), 'Middle East Technology Producers', *The Middle East Journal* (Summer 2000), *Arabizing the Internet* (1998), 'Globalizing Politics and Religion in the Muslim World', *Journal of Electronic Publishing* (1996) and co-editor of *New Media in the Arab World: The Emerging Public Sphere* (1999, 2nd edn 2003) and *Reformatting Politics: Networked Communication and Global Civil Society* (2006).

Fares Braizat is an Associate Professor of Political Science, currently serving as Head of Research at the Social and Economic Survey Research Institute (SESRI) at Qatar University. Before joining SESRI in June 2009, he served as a senior polling advisor on the Lebanese election of 2009. He also served as the deputy director and a researcher at the Center for Strategic Studies at the University of Jordan – Amman 2007–9. Prior to that he was on a Fulbright-American Political Science Association Congressional fellowship serving on the House Committee on Foreign Affairs, January–August 2007. He was a Senior Fellow at the Center for Strategic and International Studies in Washington, DC in 2006. Also, between 2003 and 2006 he served as the coordinator of the Public Opinion Polling Unit at CSS. He received his PhD in Politics and Government and his MA in Political Sociology from the University of Kent at Canterbury. Dr Braizat has published extensively on public opinion in the Arab World. He published on Muslims and democracy in the *International Journal of Comparative Sociology*, writing on how Arabs perceive the West, democracy in Jordan, governments' performances and other topics. He serves on the scientific committee of the World Values Survey and as a PI of the Arab Democracy Barometer. He is a frequent commentator for the media on public opinion and Arab affairs.

Khalid Hajji holds a BA in English Literature from Mohamed 1st University, Faculty of the Humanities, in Oujda, Morocco (his BA monograph titled 'Lemchaheb: A Socio–Cultural Phenomenon' and focusing on a group of Moroccan traditional song-makers). Additionally, he holds an MA in English Literature, from the Sorbonne University in Paris (his MA monograph being titled 'Linguistic Mechanisms and Emotional Message in Thomas Hardy's Poetry'). Dr Hajji's PhD is in Anglo-American Studies, his thesis having covered Thomas Edward Lawrence and the experience of the desert. Currently Dr Hajji serves as co-editor of *Almunaataf*, a quarterly Moroccan magazine which is known for its new approaches to themes such as the issue of women today, development and renaissance. He is a founding member of AMECLUF (Association Marocaine des Enseignants Chercheurs Laureats des Universites Francaises) and Secretary General of the Oujda Bureau of the Association. He works as a researcher in al-Jazeera Centre for Studies, and has completed over one hundred lectures in Morocco, Europe and the rest of the Arab world, in Arabic, English and French.

Fiona McCallum holds an RCUK Academic Fellowship in Religion and Politics in the School of International Relations at the University of St Andrews, Scotland. She is the author of *Christian Religious Leadership in the Middle East: The Political Role of the Patriarch* (Edwin Mellen Press, 2010) and co-founder of the Christians in the Middle East

Research Network, an initiative of the University of St Andrews and Stirling University.

Emma C. Murphy is Professor of Political Economy in the School of Government and International Affairs, University of Durham. She is a Fellow of the Royal Society for the Encouragement of Arts, Manufactures and Commerce, and a co-editor of the journal *Mediterranean Politics*. Her interests in the Arab media stem from the political economy of information and communication technology and she has published articles on this subject in journals such as *Third World Quarterly* and *International Studies Quarterly*. Her monographs include *Economic and Political Change in Tunisia: From Bourguiba to Ben Ali* (Palgrave, 1999) and (co-authored with Clive Jones) *Israel: Challenges to Identity, Democracy and the State* (Routledge, 2002).

Andreas Musolff is Professor of German at Durham University. His books include *Metaphor and Political Discourse* (2004), *Mirror Images of Europe* (2000) and *Krieg gegen die Öffentlichkeit,* (1996, on public debates about terrorism in France, Britain and Germany); he has also published three co-edited volumes on the comparative study of British and German political discourse, as well as numerous articles on metaphor theory and political communication.

Saima Saeed is an academician, media person and film-maker with research interests in the following areas of media studies: media democracy and pluralism, communication for social development, media policy and the history of media. Prior to her current engagement as a lecturer at the Centre for Culture, Media & Governance, at the Jamia Millia Islamia (a central university), New Delhi, she worked with leading television news channels in India.

Ahmet Uysal graduated from the Middle East Technical University in Ankara. He received his doctoral degree in Sociology from Southern Illinois University in 2003. His dissertation analysed the fall of Turkey's

Islamic Welfare Party from power from a social movement perspective and explored the prospect that the AK Party's reconciliation of Islam and democracy would succeed in Turkey. Dr Uysal is an Associate Professor of Sociology in the Eskisehir Osmangazi University, Turkey. He is currently studying Middle Eastern Affairs with a special focus on Turkish–Arab relations. He also speaks English, Arabic and French.

Abdel-mutaleb Al-Zuweiri is a PhD candidate in English Language at Durham University.

Mahjoob Zweiri is an Assistant Professor in Contemporary History of the Middle East at the College of Arts and Sciences at Qatar University. He was, until recently, Senior Researcher in Middle East Politics and Iran at the Center for Strategic Studies (CSS) at the University of Jordan. He is the author of numerous peer-reviewed papers, and is the co-author (with A. Ehteshami) of two books, *Iran and the Rise of Its Neoconservatives: The Politics of Tehran's Silent Revolution* (I.B. Tauris, 2007) and *Iran's Foreign Policy: From Khatami to Ahmadinejad* (Ithaca Press, 2008).

Introduction

Mahjoob Zweiri and Emma C. Murphy

The Arab world is in the midst of a new media revolution. The range of satellite television, digital media and radio programming sources is unprecedented, offering ever-expanding opportunities for the exercise of consumer choice, as well as the proliferation of diverse messages and narratives from which audiences can select. State monopolies over mass communications have been rapidly eroded, posing new challenges for censorship regimes, as well as introducing a competitive environment in which new, private sector players are seeking a growing share of the productive, promotional and distributive action.

A wealth of new research has demonstrated that this evolving media-scape is fundamentally altering the relationship between Arab publics and their governments, although the precise nature and extent of the impact on audiences remains opaque. The initial impulse to focus attention on the proliferation of the messages to which Arab audiences were suddenly being exposed has thankfully given way to a more nuanced attentiveness to audience responses, reflecting the heterogeneity of Arab populations themselves, as well as the diversity of national experiences. The rate at which different technologies embed, the spillover of one technology into another, and the tendency for message migration across media formats, vary significantly between countries. The wealthier states may not surprisingly have been the quickest off the mark when it came to 'buying in' the new media but some of the most progressive national responses have come from cash-strapped states like Egypt and Jordan, which are eager to exploit the possibilities of developing digitally savvy labour forces.

If the sensitivities of regimes and their regulatory or censorial tendencies are diverse, so too are the socially embedded cultural responses that shape and motivate audience choice. The new media are exposing the vulnerabilities of the Arab world, its political immobilism, economic stagnation and ideological insecurities, by airing challenging discourses that are both imported and surfacing from within. There has been a democratization of narrative authority as the new technologies offer a platform to anyone who has the pre-existing skills to utilize them. While some welcome the opportunities to challenge existing structures and orthodoxies, others are deeply fearful of what may turn into a form of anarchy, the loss of the region's cultural integrity and a diminishment of its distinctive identities. Citizens now have access to a range of forums that offer alternative social visions. They can listen to or participate in discussions of previously socially taboo subjects; social issues such as contraception and reproduction, critiques or advocacy of polygamy, and questioning of the prohibition on premarital sex are now discussed on satellite programmes, often aired late in the evening but increasingly finding their way into programmes targeting particular audiences such as women and youth.

Nowhere is this challenge more profoundly felt than in the religious domain, where Islam is being constantly reinvented through the multiplication of voices claiming authority and authenticity. There is now a veritable cacophony of Muslim tele-evangelists, religious advisors and official *ulema*, competing for air-time or web-space to project their version of Islam onto Arab publics and gather recruits for their visions.

The new media technologies allow traditional hierarchies to be bypassed, not least those determined by age. This is, after all, a revolution in which the young have an advantage, growing up in a digital environment that remains new and alien to many of their elders. The demographic profiles of the Arab world reflect a general disinclination on the part of either regimes or societies to grasp the nettle of managed population growth for the best part of the last fifty years. The result is rapidly expanding and increasingly youthful populations with diminishing prospects for the kind of economic growth that can satisfy their aspirations and expectations (if not their basic needs in some cases). In the absence of meaningful institutional avenues for political participation, the new media already shows signs of becoming the mechanism for youth mobilization through new social movements that organize themselves online, often drawing together diverse ideological trends in a common effort to get their voices heard and engage regimes in 'virtual' warfare which all too frequently spills over into real-world arrests and detentions.

INTRODUCTION

Interestingly, thus far such activities have largely retained their national dimensions despite the transnational nature and potential of the technologies (think of the Kifiyah movement in Egypt or the Cedar Revolution in Lebanon), despite the emergence of what Marc Lynch has identified as an Arab public. Similarly, the Arab Media Charter is less of an international regulatory institution and more a collective agreement between member states of the Arab League endorsing the sovereign rights of regimes to 'police' the media as they choose within their own borders. The ambiguities of what is national and what is transnational in this new media environment remain relatively unexplored.

An equally hard-to-measure but nonetheless crucial dimension of this revolution is its impact on relations between the Arab world and the West. The media plays a profound role in producing and reproducing identities of self and other, identities that underpin discourses of both integration and conflict within and beyond the region. The new media have become ideational battlefields on which competing political, religious, economic and social narratives are fighting it out for the Arab heart and mind, shaping perceptions of the world beyond Arab borders and articulating Arab voices for projection into that wider realm. Correspondingly, the new Arab media have become the iconic faces of the Arab world for those on the outside looking in: al-Jazeera provides a global platform to contest the hegemonic worldview of American satellite television, Jihadist websites take centre-stage in the Western security consciousness, and Facebook becomes the frontline of popular political mobilization. The internationalized nature of ownership and governance regimes, the ability of digital media to permeate national borders, and the cultural hybridity that is manifested in presentational and programming formats, all serve to contribute to and complicate this evolving interactivity. Of the many implications of this new media revolution, only one is perfectly clear: the region will never be the same and nor will its conversations with the West.

This book examines these two Janus-like faces of the new media in the Middle East: its role in reflecting developments within the region as well as its function in projecting the Arab world outside of the Middle East. It is admittedly just one part of a story that finds its roots in the 1980s, first with the launching of an Arab satellite system (Arabsat) and then with the founding of the 2M cable television station in Morocco in 1989. This was the first privately funded television media enterprise in the region, a milestone given the post-independence Arab states' monopolistic domination of mass media provision. The experiment was short-lived – the Moroccan government eventually purchased a controlling share after 2M was beset with financial problems. However, a precedent had been set which was closely followed in 1990 when, following the Iraqi invasion of Kuwait, Saudi Arabia allowed the American news channel CNN to be downloaded and rebroadcast terrestrially across its borders into Iraq to offset Iraqi war propaganda. Pandora's Box was well and truly open: in 1991 the Saudi-subsidized Middle East Broadcasting Corporation (MBC), based in London, began satellite broadcasts out of Dubai, while the Egyptian company ESN took a position in a European satellite, which allowed it to broadcast across the Arab region. The two channels provided a heady mixture of news, Arabic soap operas and popular syndicated Western programming, but they were soon to be out-broadcast and out-classed by a new local competitor. After an abortive attempt to establish a BBC Arabic service in Saudi Arabia left a number of highly qualified Arab journalists available, the al-Jazeera satellite news channel was born with an initial grant from the Emir of Qatar. In the years since, the station has been praised as a harbinger of democratic values in the region and criticized as a mouthpiece for violent extremists in the West. It has been a standard-bearer for Arab perspectives on global news issues but its journalists have been banned in just about every Arab capital at one time or another. It has remapped the world of global news interest to bring greater prominence to the problems of the south, and has itself literally become a victim of the aggressions of the north. It has brought new levels of professionalism (both in format and in journalistic conduct) to the Arab media, and been condemned by the same for its subordination to a hybridized form of Westernization. Yet wherever one stands on these issues, one cannot deny that al-Jazeera has had a tremendous impact on public consciousness and political dialogue in the Arab world. Notably, it has spawned a whole new generation of privately owned sister channels, competing to broadcast news and other formats in Arabic to the Arab world. Though the editorial perspectives and programming format are different across networks, they are all part of a common phenomenon in which Arabic-language media in general, and satellite television in particular, is no longer controlled by states or restricted by geography. News programming may be of particular interest to outside observers because of its contribution to evolving Arab publics, the opportunities for a thriving public sphere, and the possibilities that arise from challenges to both local political structures and globally hegemonic discourses. However, a whole range of new entertainment formats have also made their way into and across the region; reality television, interactive game shows, and call-up discussions, all of which encourage new forms of social participation with enticing possibilities. If millions can vote by telephone for a contestant in *Pop Idol*, how else can the potential of television be harnessed for popular action? Equally, the importation of Western television products on a massive scale (largely because this is cheaper than local production) brings new lifestyles into the Arab household, new aspirations and new fears. The global diffusion of programming mirrors the international capital networks that fund the privately owned channels, drawing the Arab world more tightly into the web (forgive the pun) of technology-driven capitalism, offering both subordination *and* opportunity. This is the frontline of globalization – politically, economically, socially and culturally.

The advent of the Internet has had a similar affect on the region. The World Wide Web first became publicly available in the Middle East in Kuwait in 1994, prior to which it had only been available in selected universities in the Gulf Arab states. By the end of the 1990s, all the Gulf Arab states were online, but the technology has been relatively slow to spread throughout the rest of the region and is still differentially accessible. Early usage was hampered not just by cost but also by the low rate at which Arabic-language websites were developed. Regimes have been reluctant to license independent service providers and many have been more concerned with controlling the available content through filtering mechanisms than with strategic development of the technology for economic purposes (Tunisia, Kuwait, Egypt and Jordan being the most forward-thinking in that sense). As small private firms have taken the initiative in developing Arabic-language software products, and as the introduction of the Internet into classroom activities has taken root, so usage (where there is access) has blossomed, although there is still evidence of a preference for educational, entertainment and networking opportunities rather than the hardcore business engagement that is needed for the development of a true knowledge-economy. Interesting studies of business preferences indicate problems with trust in the technology, while the Arab Human Development Reports have provided harsh indictments of the political and cultural 'blocks' that inhibit the building of a knowledge-based society in the Arab world and lead regimes to place emphasis on government-to-citizen electronic communications rather than real interactivity. But the Internet is a virtuous technology insofar as it provides the means itself for governmental and social restrictions to be evaded. Subjects that national governments find too controversial for local newspapers can easily be published on a number of popular or personal weblog forums. Blogging has arguably become the predominant form of written protest and social commentary; the Internet is becoming the region's new clandestine printing press.

Radio too has benefited from these private sector innovations. As a technology, it is perhaps the most transportable and, in some areas, remains the most accessed. It is perhaps not as glamorous as its visual counterpart, television, but the set-up costs are lower, making it a more accessible medium for small-scale enterprises such as civil society organizations or local endeavours. The interactive formats of television and the Internet have migrated to radio, offering listeners participatory opportunities and turning it into a reflective mirror of localized social concerns, in turn giving new significance to the local in relation to the national or even the global.

Of course, these three media technologies – satellite television, radio and the Internet – form only a part of the new media infrastructure of today. The technologies do not stand alone but are increasingly integrated and interdependent. Television and radio stations have web-based dimensions: they can be accessed through the Internet and usually have web-based accompaniments. GSM technology means broadcasts can be downloaded through mobile phones anywhere and everywhere, and the same technologies allow for portability and interactivity in even the remotest locations. Thus it is dauntingly evident that the impact of the new media revolution is multi-tiered and multi-dimensional to such an extent, and in such a rapidly evolving manner, that capturing any sense of its impact is inevitably a limited exercise. Moreover, the proliferation of media outlets and the search for market shares has encouraged television and radio channels and websites to reach out to previously neglected demographics in a new way. Audiences are fragmented and segmented, by gender, religiosity, age, geography, ethnicity, orientation – to such an extent that we have to ask 'which' audience is being impacted upon. Just because greater political awareness is now only a few clicks of a remote control away does not guarantee that all viewers will be interested, let alone that they will all respond similarly. The democratizing potential of the new media environment may yet be subverted by the diversity and contrariness of audiences as much as by captive business classes connected umbilically to regime elites, conservative religious hierarchies or the sheer anarchy of the media landscape.

However, it is not only hopes for a democratizing impact that sustain interest in the new media. The technologies allow for dialogue, for representation and conversation between, as much as within, cultures and political systems. The Arab world gazes on a Western media environment that is enviably both pluralist and liberal, but that is equally beset with 'interested' connections between political and economic power, which manifests itself in global hypocrisies. The Western gaze towards the Arab media sees both possibilities for democratization through the back door of media discourses and the potential for radicalization through 'irresponsible' messaging. In the aftermath of 9/11, al-Jazeera became a lightning rod for US government angst at the Arab media due to its airing, in full, of messages from Osama Bin Laden. Thus the media becomes not only the medium but also the voice itself. It is hardly surprising then that, recognizing the influence of these outlets, the US has become increasingly concerned with how it is portrayed in the Arab new media. Though the US-government-sponsored Arabic satellite network, al-Hurra, has proved ineffectual, it is important to note that one of President Barack Obama's first acts in office was to appear on al-Arabiya for a sit-down interview. The new media indeed may widen the gap in perception between East and West, but in other ways it holds the potential to bring these areas closer together.

As this introduction has suggested, there are an infinite variety of avenues to explore when assessing the new media revolution in the Arab region. This book began as a conference at the University of Durham in 2007 focused on addressing media issues in the post-9/11 Middle East. It is clear that any serious discussion of the future of the region, its politics, its economics and its social movements, cannot move forward without incorporating an analysis of the media and its impact. With that in mind, we believe that this book provides a valuable introduction and analysis of some of the important issues surrounding this new media revolution.

We start with the iconic satellite television channel that in many ways is emblematic of that revolution. The first chapter discusses editorial differences across al-Jazeera's English- and Arabic-language content. Al-Jazeera continues to play a major role today in Middle Eastern and international politics, as it is increasingly recognized by international audiences as a reliable source of news while expressing a pan-Arab orientation. It causes major problems for the policies of the United States and current Arab governments in the region. This chapter argues that al-Jazeera in Arabic and al-Jazeera International display significant differences in their approach and content. By conducting a content analysis of al-Jazeera's TV channels and websites, the study maintains that the differences in content can be attributed to editorial preference and the type of format. Analysing the framing of the Turkish presidential crises of mid-2007, it finds that there were significant differences in the coverage of the crises between al-Jazeera outlets and that these differences can be attributed to editorial preference and audience characteristics, reflecting the tendency of globalizing processes to 'produce' messages rather than simply relay them. As al-Jazeera continues to advance its global rather than solely regional status, it will be interesting to see how its message frames adapt accordingly.

The second chapter addresses the role of the Internet in the Middle East. It suggests that, as a media format, the Internet is not really liberating, nor even very democratic; a strong state is not required to dash such hopes. As a composite technology, the Internet spills across established institutions and arrangements; thus actual Internet implantation in the Middle East occasioned a new round of state–society bargaining, which constitutes the real politics of the Internet. Drawing on comparative studies conducted in Egypt, Jordan, Syria and Saudi Arabia, this chapter outlines alliance-seeking, reputation management and the shift of reference groups that constructed its social infrastructure, accompanied at the micro level by the emergence of new elites and at the macro level by a shift in the political economy of development from modernization to globalization.

The third chapter explores the media vocabulary used to discuss the war in Iraq. This chapter sheds light on the way the media structured public awareness of the Iraq war by using common metaphors. Specifically, it looks at the metaphor of *passing a milestone* as a reference to the political/military 'progress' in the Iraq war since April 2003. A corpus of Iraq war news on CNN and al-Jazeera is analysed by applying the method of cognitive metaphor analysis. The data indicates that the *milestone* metaphor is used in three different scenarios, each of which is politically loaded in order to express a particular perspective on the war and its future outcome. The distribution of the three different scenarios is further interpreted as an indication of the degree to which the US administration's perspective appears to be dominating the international perception of the war.

The fourth chapter discusses perception as shaped by the media. The media is a for-profit industry, and currently terror sells. The twentieth century will go down in history for making wars a mass-mediated phenomenon. In 1916 the Creel Commission 'manufactured consent' for the First World War, and, years later, elites in the United States believed that 'Vietnam Syndrome' had to be cured. By the time the Gulf War occurred, no questions were asked, and many attributed this phenomenon to the 'CNN effect'.

Modern media with its 'annihilation of space and time' lends a sense of urgency to wartime reporting. Powerful news organizations exhibit their technological *tour de force* by airing events 'live' as they unfold, extending the terror of the front into the home. Through the post-9/11 oversaturation of 'terror videos', the Middle East became an important 'beat' for world media. As this one event changed the relationship between the Middle East and the West it opened fresh debates. Have the media ended up reinforcing stereotypes leading to 'Islamophobia'? Are media representations often constructed in relation to which side of the fence one stands, reflecting President Bush's infamous words: 'You're either with us or against us'? Worst still, is the media, instead of questioning this logic, becoming instrumental in furthering the 'just war' argument, resulting in Habermasian 'refeudalization of the public sphere'? And, by doing so, is the media's own transformatory potential becoming doubtful?

The fifth chapter addresses the construction of images of the other in the media. This chapter contends that the polarized vision of the world typical of 'Clash of Civilizations' theories is not productive in terms of meaning. It follows that there is an urgent need to outgrow the limits of the traditional prisms of looking at the reality of the relations between the West and the Arab/Islamic world. It is a truism that the established media system, both in the West and in the Arab world, plays a major role in shaping the images of the self, the other and the world, and, consequently, decides on the future of the relation between them.

Unless the media system changes, the theories of a clash of civilizations will continue to wreak havoc.

It is difficult to imagine any headway on the path to reform of the media system without a fundamental critique of the 'image culture' and a reassessment of its role in launching dialogue or exacerbating conflict. This study aims to shed light on some hidden cultural, philosophical and historical dimensions of this image culture, dimensions meant to alert the reader to the following facts: the dominant image culture is part of a dominant culture of hegemony, and the dominant image culture is a harbinger of the End of Media.

Are there alternatives to the decaying media system in both the Arab and Western worlds? The second part of the study rethinks the role of media in its relation to the concept of 'mediation'. Only a media system conscious of its role as mediator can avert publics from the suicidal path to which they are invited by the dominant image culture. Another necessary concept worthy of exploration is 'out-formation', as opposed to 'in-formation'.

The sixth chapter seeks to address the implications of the spread of the new media on Middle Eastern politics by examining the experience of the Coptic community. The Copts are an indigenous group located in Egypt whose significant distinguishing feature from the Muslim majority is their Christian faith. A relatively large diaspora community lives beyond Egypt and the new technologies have provided a revolution in the channels and formats of communication between them, which have in turn impacted upon their relationship with wider Egyptian society and the Egyptian regime. This case study offers an enticing alternative vision of how the relationships between 'inside' and 'outside' that are manifested through the new media technologies can include relationships within a single community, as well as how the technologies are themselves generating new dynamics in relations between citizens and the state.

The seventh chapter explores the tensions between two alternative understandings of how contemporary media-based Information Communication Technologies (ICTs) are impacting upon state–society relations. A growing body of research on the Arab media draws upon the Habermasian notion of a public sphere, built upon communicative action, which sees an autonomous public contesting and challenging the structures of the state. This is a vision for democratization and contrasts strongly with post-structuralist media theses that place greater emphasis on the colonizing effects of media capitalism and the subordination of the individual to the production and promotion of lifestyle rather than material reality. This chapter suggests that there exists a dialectical reciprocity between the image and reality of a public sphere, which is itself the potential source for political change in the Arab world but which is unlikely to generate the structural changes to which democrats aspire.

The eighth chapter delves into a discussion of differences between media audiences in the Middle East. Between 2003 and 2008, self-reported Internet usage and satellite-dish ownership has increased significantly in Jordan. These developments allow for greater access to sources of information on domestic politics and comparative perspectives on political development that are not constrained by traditional state-influenced outlets. This chapter compares domestic political perception held by Jordanians who identify al-Jazeera Television as their primary source of news against those who continue to receive the majority of their news from al-Arabiya or Jordanian Television. Controlling for demographic variables, this chapter makes progress towards isolating the effects of the Arab world's new media environment on Jordanian political attitudes.

The final chapter assesses the role and impact of the rapidly emerging media sector in Jordan. In particular it will consider the potential of the radio to play a role in increasing participation and political engagement and it will discuss technological proliferation, which is central to the Millennium Development Goals (MDGs).

The summaries offered above may bemuse the reader with their sheer range but we make no apology for the disparate aspects of new media impact that we have included: they reflect the vastness of research that has been engendered by the subject and that was evidenced by the breadth of coverage offered for inclusion in the original conference. To try to bring such diversity into a single meta-frame would be to 'force a round peg into a square hole', and would necessarily exclude the very multi-dimensionalism that is evidenced by the new media revolution itself. The chapters in this book address multiple issues that we believe are critical *but not sufficient* to understanding the impact, scope, difficulties and opportunities presented by the new media revolution in the Middle East. By approaching this phenomenon from many different angles, we hope the book provides a critical and analytical basis from which to explore some aspects of the changing Middle Eastern media scene, but we are the first to acknowledge that this is but a drop in the ocean of the research that is needed before we can fully comprehend what is probably the most significant development in the Arab region since the emergence of the independent state.

Amman, March 2009

1

The New Frontier in International Politics: The Nature of al-Jazeera's Prime-time Broadcasting in Arabic and English

Ahmet Uysal

Introduction

The mass media play a significant role in modern politics at both national and international levels. Some scholars have even defined the mass media and new communications tools as the fourth estate, arguing that, since the structuring of modern society no more requires face-to-face political communication between rulers and people, the mass media has become the major outlet for political communication. The mass media can shape relationships between the first three powers, i.e., the legislature, the executive and the judiciary. When a political system faces problems in the functioning of these three powers, the media plays a strong and critical role in what several scholars have defined as a new type of 'mediated politics'.[1] This also seems to be the case for international politics in the New World Order that took shape after the collapse of the Soviet bloc in 1989.

The New World Order/Disorder, which was marked by the first Gulf War, brought with it a new medium of political communication. The broadcasting of the live images of the Allied Forces' bombing Iraq by American channel CNN in a sense carried the war directly into the houses of millions around the world for the first time in history. In a way, CNN was confirming US leadership in the newly shaped world politics. However, this unipolar world order was not free of problems. The free flow of information challenged the one-sided discourses of national governments from within and without. The rise of Islamic fundamentalism in general and al-Qaeda in particular posed major challenges to American (or Western) interests, culminating in the attacks of 11 September 2001. America's subsequent waging of wars against Afghanistan and Iraq were components of its response to these challenges and its efforts to strengthen American interests and influence in the world. In the second Iraq War, too, journalists were 'embedded' into the American troops to report and broadcast the invasion (or liberation) of Iraq, symbolizing the 'mediated' nature of these new world politics.

Meanwhile, the launching of Qatar's al-Jazeera TV in 1996 had also marked a new stage in regional Middle Eastern and international politics. On the one hand, it allowed the voices of the previously silent masses to be heard, challenging the communicative monopoly of the authoritarian Arab regimes in the region. On the other, these voices were often also of those who rejected the unipolar New World Order led by the United States. Al-Jazeera's successful broadcasting in Arabic dethroned CNN and the BBC as the main international disseminators of news in the Arabic-speaking world. Moreover, this challenge was carried to the English-speaking world by the launching of al-Jazeera International broadcasting in English last year.

In this chapter, I will argue that al-Jazeera's Arabic and English versions show a significant divergence in terms of content and approach. I will argue that the Arabic broadcasting tends to display a more Third World and pan-Arab orientation, while its English counterpart tends to display a more international approach. This implies that, despite the common ownership, the editorial preferences and audience expectations play out in shaping the choice and portrayal of the news in the global and regional scales. I also compare al-Jazeera's news coverage on its websites to that on its television channels. This enables us to argue that the format of news coverage in written and visual forms can also influence the content and form of the coverage. To display these differences, I conducted a content analysis on the prime-time news for a whole week on al-Jazeera Arabic and English for the same dates (on television and websites) in order to explain the nature of the news reporting as well as their framing of the news. More specifically, in order to show the difference between the Arabic and international (English) version, I analyse their coverage of the crisis of the Turkish presidential elections in late April 2007.

Al-Jazeera: a different story of new global politics

Modern politics is more and more shaped by mass communication tools. Unlike previous eras, today's transnational broadcasters do not need the consent of a national government to address its native citizens, thus limiting the state's monopoly over the definition of reality in that particular country. Thus, for quite some time, satellite television has been seen as a challenge to national cultures and sovereignty,[2] not least because it may address an entire geocultural region.[3] For proponents of this view, those who share a common language and culture across countries constitute a unique potential market. For example, from Azerbaijan to Germany the population that speaks the Turkish language constitutes the geocultural region. Those who conceptualize the effects of the mass media through terms such as 'deterritorialization'[4] and 'displacement'[5] imply that international communication tools curtail people's commitment to their national territorial relations and identities, making it harder for the states to assimilate or integrate native or immigrant minorities. For that reason, some have even claimed that, because it has escaped the negative effects of state control, al-Jazeera can be understood as a counter-hegemonic force challenging the existing political order and its prevalent social discourse.[6]

Every significant change is also likely to face resistance and reaction from those who are challenged by its cultural, political or economical consequences. The Middle East region's socio-political characteristics (i.e., the authoritarian regimes, civil strife, terrorism, Israeli–Arab conflict and American interventions) all generate oppositional voices, and the arrival of al-Jazeera represented a window for the airing of such voices. The Qatari Emir's (Hamad Bin Khalifa al-Thani's) decision to launch al-Jazeera had coincided with the closure of the BBC Arabic channel, enabling the new channel to hire the quality journalists who had become available.[7] Literally meaning the 'Arabian Peninsula', al-Jazeera became the first Arabic-language channel to be directly critical of Arab regimes while being located on Arab soil.[8] For Naomi Sakr, the government's reason for launching the station was to use it as a foreign policy tool, compensating for Qatar's small size and having little to lose in so doing.[9] The Qatari government allocated to the channel management a large five-year loan and editorial freedom, which was missing in other regional broadcasting companies. It is believed that the government also secures al-Jazeera's financial operations against shortfalls, although the company is still generally viewed as a privately owned channel.[10] The editorial freedom it enjoys is unique in the region, allowing it to cover issues formerly considered taboo (e.g., sexuality and corruption). With a high-tech structure and flashy presentation, the channel also provides a visual experience to the viewers. Thus al-Jazeera's success lay in a combination of several critical advantages such as 'secure funds, live uncensored programming, free-to-air, analogue [and digital] twenty-four-hour transmission'.[11] Today, al-Jazeera remains as a 'valid and a reliable source' of news recognized by the Western media and a challenger to the throne of CNN.[12] For example, a Google search for al-Jazeera yields about 40,000 results on the *New York Times* website (nytimes.com) compared to 8,000 each on the CNN and BBC websites. In other words, the leading news outlets widely cite al-Jazeera as a popular source of news.

In spite of this, like Arab governments, the American government has not been pleased with al-Jazeera's coverage of the wars in Afghanistan and Iraq, and has publicly criticized the station's broadcasting of video footage of Osama Bin Laden and other anti-American groups. Dramatically, the station's office in Iraq was bombed by the American forces several times and the US-appointed Iraqi Governing Council excluded al-Jazeera from its press conferences for inciting people to murder American soldiers.[13] The al-Jazeera English-language website was even hacked into and an image of the American flag posted on the site.[14]

Programming

In contrast to the region's government-controlled TV stations, al-Jazeera has emphasized the principle of providing diverse opinions and counter-opinions. In doing so, it has forced other Arab media stations such as Abu Dhabi TV to open up their own strictly controlled broadcasting and follow its provocative style. In that sense, al-Jazeera created a new public space for open discussion that was previously missing in the region.[15] When we look at the main programmes on al-Jazeera, they reflect its unique approach to news coverage in the region. (Notably, two of the channel's mottos are 'opinion and counter-opinion' and 'a platform for those without a platform'.) The channel broadcasts both live and recorded programmes. The live programme *Al-Ittijah al-Muakis* (*The Opposite Direction*) is one of the most popular, with a vast array of issues being discussed by opposing parties.[16] In May 2007, for example, topics broadcasted included 'Reform and Change in the Middle East', 'Arab Oil: A Blessing or a Curse', 'Arab Youth and the Problems of the Nation' and 'Violence in Western and Arab Countries'. The programme and its participants frequently criticize Arab governments, sometimes creating diplomatic problems for Qatar.[17] In 2002, for example, the Saudi government boycotted regional meetings in Qatar and refused visas for the al-Jazeera crew because of its critical stand.[18] However, governments' complaints about al-Jazeera's coverage of political and social issues in their own countries[19] have incited the response from the Qatari government that the channel is a private venture and the government does not have any control over its content and operation.

Other live programmes have included *More than an Opinion*, *Without Limits*, *Open Dialogue*, *Religion and Life*, *Beyond the News*, *al-Jazeera Platform*, *The American Presidential Race*, and *From Washington*. All the programme names imply the unconventional nature of al-Jazeera. Programmes such as *Religion and Life*, hosted by the famous Egyptian cleric Yousef al-Qaradawi, are conducted in an interactive mode by allowing the viewers to call in and voice their opinions or ask sensitive questions. The recorded programmes also address critical and controversial issues regarding history, politics, culture, the economy and health. Among them is the programme *With Heikal*, in which Muhammed Hassanein Heikal, a leading Arab nationalist and scholar of Middle Eastern politics, discusses modern Arab and international politics. It has to be said that in its political coverage al-Jazeera is not always neutral. On the issue of Arab–Israeli conflict, al-Jazeera's sympathetic attitude towards the Palestinians is obvious but it nonetheless gives airtime to, and conducts interviews with, proponents of both sides of the conflict.

Al-Jazeera has itself faced a growing challenge from some new Arab channels such as al-Arabiya, MBC (Middle East Broadcasting Center), and Abu Dhabi TV, which have tried to emulate al-Jazeera's success. Al-Jazeera has responded by carrying its own mission into the international arena through the launch of al-Jazeera International in 2006, which addresses the English-speaking audience around the world. Its main rivals in the field are CNN and the BBC, and the new English-language channel has recruited various renowned journalists such as Riz Khan and David Frost, who formerly worked for them. The most popular programmes on the channel are *People and Power*, which claims to investigate the 'use and abuse of power';[20] *The Riz Khan Show*, which allows an audience to ask questions of news-makers directly;[21] *Witness*, which focuses on human stories and provocative debates; *Frost Over The World*, hosted by David Frost; and *101 East*, which focuses on Asian affairs. These programmes are highly interactive and have a more general and international focus than those on al-Jazeera's Arabic outlet. Subscribers can also watch the channel online.

Media framing: a content analysis of al-Jazeera's news coverage

The mass media constitute a major symbolic arena in which rival groups and individuals compete to establish the accepted definition of reality.[22] Framing is a concept that analyses the process of claim-making on various issues in society and politics. Robert Entman defined the concept as 'making some aspects of reality more salient in a text in order to promote a particular "problem definition", causal interpretation, moral evaluation and/or treatment recommendation for the item described'.[23] Media framing provides 'patterns of cognition, interpretation, and presentation, of selection, emphasis, and exclusion, by which symbol-handlers routinely organize discourse, whether verbal or visual'.[24] This framing plays a significant role in defining controversial issues, by covering the events in a certain way, by magnifying certain of their aspects and emphasizing others, and by providing legitimacy to various actors. The way the mass media frame issues is affected by various factors such as the source of information, the control over transmission, or the material and ideological interests of journalists.[25] While no one denies their significant role in public debates, it remains an open question whether the media reflects public opinion or is itself a mechanism to influence it. In other words, the media's selection and presentation of an event or an issue can have significant consequences in public debates. This chapter aims to analyse al-Jazeera's news coverage on its television channels and websites. Each of al-Jazeera's media outlets consists of both an English- and Arabic-language version. For the purpose of this study, I try here to compare and contrast al-Jazeera's different formats, i.e., its Arabic and English versions along with the television and web-based formats. Specifically, I focus on three themes: news topics, level of coverage and area of coverage.

To ascertain the nature of the news topics covered on al-Jazeera's television channels and websites, I analysed 258 news items collected over a four-day period for al-Jazeera's television channels and a five-day period for web coverage during the second half of May 2007. To be more precise, the news was taken from the dates 18, 23, 25, 28 and 29 May 2007 from the Arabic- and English-language websites, while the television news was taken from the hourly news programming on 23, 24, 25 and 27 May 2007. The television news was taken from the 30-minute prime-time news hour (i.e., 5.00–5.30 p.m. on al-Jazeera International and 6.00 and 6.30 p.m. on al-Jazeera Arabic). The web news was collected from the front page of the Arabic- and English-language websites.

A vast array of topics was covered on al-Jazeera's four different outlets. The classification offered below summarizes the types of topics covered in the period examined. As can be seen in Table 1.1, a major portion of the total news is political news, including 40.7 per cent of total 'stories'. A quarter of stories cover the military news – the fighting and wars then taking place in the Middle East. Twelve per cent of the news stories focused on economic affairs around the world and 10 per cent on domestic or civil strife within different regions. There was meagre coverage of other types of news on al-Jazeera as a whole.

TABLE 1.1
News topics on al-Jazeera

Topics	TV		Web		Total	
	#	%	#	%	#	%
Political	40	41.2	65	40.4	105	40.7
Military	32	33.0	34	21.1	66	25.6
Economic	7	7.2	24	14.9	31	12.0
Civil Strife	12	12.4	14	8.7	26	10.1
Cultural	3	3.1	16	9.9	19	7.4
Disasters	3	3.1	3	1.9	6	2.3
Others	0	0.0	5	3.1	5	1.9
Total	97	100.0	161	100.0	258	100.0

When the coverage of television and website news is compared, political and military news seems to dominate the television news, with 41.2 and 33 per cent of stories respectively. However, the web news seems to have had a little more balanced distribution. Considered separately, the weight of political news remained about the same on each type of format. However, the economic news seems to have found twice as much space on the websites than on the television. Military news and civil strife found more space for themselves on television than on the websites, due probably to the more sensationalist nature of news coverage on television. In addition, the format of a website allows more freedom and space to cover a variety of issues, something which is less easy for news coverage on the TV where the major news events dominate the agenda of the day.

By looking at whether the news focused on a local issue that concerned a single country or on a wider area, I further classified the news covered on al-Jazeera as local, pan-Arab or international. A news item about a single country or national community is coded as 'local'. When the news addresses an issue that concerns two or more Arab countries it is classified as 'pan-Arab', and a news account about any two countries, at least one of which is not Arab, is classified as 'international'. Viewed as a whole, the major portion of the news (40.7 per cent) covered on al-Jazeera is found to concern a single country or community (see Table 1.2). A third of the news (32.9 per cent) covered relations between Arab countries or communities, and about a quarter (26.4 per cent) dealt with international news.

TABLE 1.2
Level of news coverage

Levels	TV		Web		Total	
	#	%	#	%	#	%
Local	36	37.1	69	42.9	105	40.7
Pan-Arab	44	45.4	41	25.5	85	32.9
International	17	17.5	51	31.7	68	26.4
Total	97	100.0	161	100.0	258	100.0

The picture becomes more interesting when television and web coverage are considered separately. While the pan-Arab news constitutes a little less than half the news (45.4 per cent), it contributes just a quarter of the news (25.5 per cent) on the website where local news constitutes the majority (see Table 1.2). In other words, the television coverage has a more Arab emphasis than the web coverage.

The study also coded the news according to the geographical region of the globe that was being discussed. As shown in Table 1.3, about a half of the total news coverage concerned the events and issues in the Middle East region (51.6 per cent). Again there is a significant difference between coverage on television and on the web. While news of the Middle East constitutes about two-thirds of the television news, this is reduced to less than half the coverage on the website (64.9 and 43.5 per cent respectively). Television coverage deals with other regions in a roughly equivalent manner. However, a quarter of al-Jazeera's web news focused on Asia, indicating close attention to the region also reflected in the fact that al-Jazeera has a major branch in Kuala Lumpur, Malaysia.

TABLE 1.3
Area of coverage

Areas	TV		Web		Total	
	#	%	#	%	#	%
Middle East	63	64.9	70	43.5	133	51.6
Asia	11	11.3	39	24.2	50	19.4
Europe	12	12.4	16	9.9	28	10.9
North America	2	2.1	14	8.7	16	6.2
Africa	6	6.2	13	8.1	19	7.4
Other	3	3.1	9	5.6	12	4.7
Total	97	100.0	161	100.0	258	100.0

Arabic- and English-language coverage

I have shown that there was a significant difference between al-Jazeera's television and website news coverage. When the news that appeared on al-Jazeera outlets was studied, significant differences also appeared in the topics covered during the period covered (see Table 1.4). While the political topics on both outlets remained similar, military issues seemed to be covered more widely in the Arabic-language news than in its English counterparts (35.4 per cent versus 21.0 per cent). Specifically, the Arabic-language television channel and website both focused on the various conflicts within the Middle East. In contrast, economic news seems to have found twice as much space in English-language outlets than in Arabic ones (14.2 and 7.3 per cent respectively). Arabic prime-time television news and website front pages did not cover any cultural events, but the same was not true for English versions, where 10.8 per cent of news items related to cultural events.

TABLE 1.4
News topics by broadcasting/publishing language

Topics	Arabic		English		Total	
	#	%	#	%	#	%
Political	36	43.9	69	39.2	105	40.7
Military	29	35.4	37	21.0	66	25.6
Economic	6	7.3	25	14.2	31	12.0
Civil Strife	9	11.0	17	9.7	26	10.1
Cultural	0	0.0	19	10.8	19	7.4
Disasters	2	2.4	4	2.3	6	2.3
Others	0	0.0	5	2.8	5	1.9
Total	82	100.0	176	100.0	258	100.0

As can be expected, the primary objective of news on the Arabic-language television channel and website was to inform a specifically Arab audience, whereas their English counterparts focus on informing the international community. This is reflected in the level of coverage of local, Arab and international news. As Table 1.5 shows, a little more than half of the Arabic-language broadcasting and publication (51.2 per cent) covered issues of particular concern to Arabs, including the Arab–Israeli conflict, the invasion of and war in Iraq, and events in Lebanon. A quarter of the news covered local events, including both individual Arab and non-Arab incidents. About half of the English-language news concerned localized events around the world (47.7 per cent). The rest of the news on both media in both languages involved events of international importance (again, see Table 1.5).

Similarly, Arabic-language coverage predominantly focused on issues in the Middle East (78 per cent – see Table 1.6). However, the English-language coverage focused much less on the Middle East (39.2 per cent) and to a greater extent on Asia.

TABLE 1.5
Level of coverage in Arabic and English language

Levels	Arabic		English		Total	
	#	%	#	%	#	%
Local	21	25.6	84	47.7	105	40.7
Pan-Arab	42	51.2	43	24.4	85	32.9
International	19	23.2	49	27.8	68	26.4
Total	82	100.0	176	100.0	258	100.0

TABLE 1.6
Area of coverage in Arabic and English

Areas	Arabic		English		Total	
	#	%	#	%	#	%
Middle East	64	78.0	69	39.2	133	51.6
Asia	5	6.1	45	25.6	50	19.4
Europe	3	3.7	25	14.2	28	10.9
Africa	4	4.9	15	8.5	19	7.4
America	3	3.7	13	7.4	16	6.2
Other	3	3.7	9	5.1	12	4.7
Total	82	100.0	176	100.0	258	100.0

As a general comment it can also be said that when broadcasting in Arabic, al-Jazeera demonstrates its oppositional or anti-Western credentials through its selection of items to cover and the language it uses (for example, labelling Hamas suicide bombers as 'martyrs' rather than using the term 'suicide bombers' as it does on English-language media). In the English-language outlets, this anti- or perhaps non-Westernism is displayed by the extensive coverage of Asian and non-Western news and cultural affairs.

Al-Jazeera on the Turkish presidential election
The possibility that the new president might be a representative of the moderate Islamic AK Party stirred huge concern on the part of secular elites and factions in Turkey in the period during which the study was

conducted. This controversial process drew attention to a number of critical issues, such as the relationship between religion and politics, the meaning of democracy, and civil–military relations in Turkey. The secular oppositions' so-called 'republican' protests gathered hundreds of thousands in the major cities, while the military issued an ultimatum to the government, and other forms of institutional resistance forced the AK Party to press for an early election, a process that drew much attention from al-Jazeera. By conducting a content analysis of the news on the presidential crisis during the second half of April and early May 2007, I tried to decipher the nature of al-Jazeera's framing of this controversial issue on its Arabic- and English-language websites.

At first sight, the number of news items that covered the Turkish presidential election in al-Jazeera Arabic seems to be not much higher than in its English twin (33 and 27 news accounts respectively). In fact, the Arabic-language website provided a more comprehensive coverage of the process than the English website, the text of the Arabic coverage reaching 30,658 words as opposed to 12,246 in the English version. The Arabic version also published the detailed transcripts of the televised debates of the process on its website. The coverage in both languages generally appeared to be balanced and neutral with the exception of two news accounts in English that seemed to favour the secular opposition to the AK Party and five news accounts in Arabic that seemed to favour the AK Party. Nonetheless, significant differences in coverage did emerge.

English-language coverage
The labels that al-Jazeera International used to portray Prime Minister Erdogan and his AK Party were interestingly diverse. They emphasized the party's Islamic roots and orientation in order to explain the causes of the crisis. In that regard, the terms 'Islamic-led',[26] 'Islamist-rooted',[27] 'Islamic-oriented'[28] and 'ex-Islamist'[29] were used to define the AK government, but it was also mentioned that the AK Party itself rejected such an Islamist label and agenda.[30]

In covering the electoral process, the secular 'republican' protests received comprehensive coverage. At the beginning of the process, secular protests in Ankara were covered in detail and were viewed as a sign of 'widening divisions between Turkey's secular and Islamist camps'.[31] Arguably, an anti-AK Party attitude was demonstrated by al-Jazeera when secularist 'republican' protests in Ankara were covered solely through the discourse of the protesters.[32] This was uncharacteristic of al-Jazeera, which generally allows all the opposing sides of disputes to voice their views. The announcement of Abdullah Gul's candidacy was framed as a positive development and al-Jazeera International mentioned the mainstream media and big business' (TUSIAD's) approval of Gul.[33]

The English-language channel associated the secular opposition and protests with the military.[34] For example, it noted the demand of the army's chief of staff, Yasar Buyukanit, for a president loyal to the republic in essence, not words.[35] On another occasion, al-Jazeera International claimed that after the secularist protests in Ankara the military took 'a more concessionist stance'.[36] At other times, the military was framed as being at the centre of the conflict and the opposition parties were labelled as secularist and pro-army.[37] In a similar vein, the military's online ultimatum/statement against the government and the controversy resulting from the crisis were widely covered by al-Jazeera International. For example, the military statement was framed as a 'secularist ultimatum' against the Islamic-oriented AK government.[38] The European and American reactions to the statement were also well noted. In explaining the role of the military in Turkish politics, and to provide a background for the crisis, the earlier military coups were mentioned and the threat of a military coup was revived as a possibility. The AK Party's rejection of the military ultimatum was described as an 'unprecedented defiance against Turkey's military generals'.[39]

Al-Jazeera's English-language website noted that the secular establishment (i.e., a coalition of the then-president, Ahmet Necdet Sezer, the military and top judges) was trying to prevent an ex-Islamist from becoming the president of Turkey.[40] The blocking of the AK Party's candidate by the Constitutional Court on the basis of technicalities was attributed to the pressure exerted by the military.[41] The Court's decision that a two-thirds attendance was required was also characterized as a 'shocking defeat' for the AK Party.[42] The AK government's decision to go for early elections was framed as an attempt 'to resolve a stand-off with the country's military'.[43] To explain the causes of this crisis it was stated that 'a growing class of prosperous and more religious-minded Turks want a relaxation of curbs on religious symbols and expression'.[44]

Arabic-language coverage
As noted above, the Arabic-language coverage of the Turkish presidential election process was a lot more extensive than the English coverage, both in terms of the number of accounts and their content. Unlike its English twin, some Arabic news accounts clearly displayed a pro-AK Party attitude but most of the reports were neutral in their coverage of the Turkish election process.

The submission of Abdullah Gul's candidacy for president and the secular protests against that prospect attracted a significant level of coverage on al-Jazeera. The Arabic site's interest in the election started earlier than the English website's, but the English version covered the 'republican protests' more extensively than the Arabic. Even before the crisis, al-Jazeera reminded its readers that the possibility of Abdullah Gul becoming the next president faced challenges from two main obstacles: the opposition Republican People's Party (RPP) and the military.[45] Buyukanıt's statement that the new president must be loyal to secularism in essence was noted several times in that context.[46]

When explaining the political struggle and civil–military relations in Turkey, al-Jazeera frequently reminded its readers about the earlier military coups that had granted the military a dominant role in the political system and suggested that the possibility of another military coup was on the table.[47] The EU and American disapproval of the military's intervention were portrayed as their taking one side in the dispute and were framed positively.[48] At one point, the UK newspaper the *Guardian* was quoted for comparing Turkey and Algeria, where the secular military was likewise trying to curb the Islamists' power.[49]

The nature of the problem in Turkey was seen in a slightly different way in the Arabic coverage. For example, in one account the presidential crisis was framed as a struggle between the AK government and the military.[50] When describing the AK Party and its leaders, emphasis was given to their Islamic orientation.[51] Another account labelled the AK Party as 'renovationist Islamists'.[52] In yet another account, an Egyptian writer defined the Turkish situation as a 'struggle of identity' and labelled the crisis as the 'destruction of the future' in Turkey.[53] Elsewhere, the crisis was framed as a struggle between Islam and secularism.[54] As for the causes of the crises, al-Jazeera on its website thought that the secular protests aimed to stop what was called 'the Islamic tide'[55] and to prevent the headscarf from entering the presidential palace.[56] However, the protests were depicted as representing the minority rather than the majority and the headscarf was projected as the primary symbol of an identity struggle in Turkey.[57]

As a sign of al-Jazeera's close interest in Turkey, the Arabic website published several detailed analytical articles by Egyptian, Jordanian and Lebanese writers about the political process in Turkey.[58] In his article, the Lebanese writer noted that Turkey was ignoring the fact that it is a Muslim state and trying to convince Europe of its secularism and Europeanism.[59]

Proclaiming the unconstitutional nature of the proceedings, the Republican People's Party (RPP) applied to the Supreme Court for the cancellation of the election's first round; the Court cancelled the ballot on the basis that the participation of 367 MPs was required to start the voting. Both the Arabic and English websites associated the Court's decision with military pressure and the secularist 'republican' protests.[60] Prime Minister Erdoğan's criticism of the Supreme Court's decision as a bullet to the heart of democracy was cited several times by both the English and Arabic versions.[61]

Conclusion

The differences in media framing between the Arabic and English al-Jazeera outlets can be attributed to editorial differences (i.e., the differences in cultural backgrounds of international and Arab journalists) as well as to the nature of the audiences. However, this study concludes that there are also differences in the content of the news coverage between the al-Jazeera television channels and the websites which can be attributed to the nature of each format. While the television news reporting is bound by a time frame (i.e., half-an-hour programming), website reporting has more freedom, is not as bound by time and space, and can also take advantage of the interactive nature of Internet technology. Moreover, the website format allows more freedom and space than television does to cover a variety of issues, major news events almost exclusively dominating each day's television agenda.

Al-Jazeera is still making news about news as it maintains its bold and provocative style of broadcasting. It is too early to determine the scope and extent of its influence long-term but it is clear that the Middle East will not be the same after al-Jazeera.

NOTES

1. Brian McNair, *Journalism and Democracy: An Evaluation of the Political Public Sphere*, London: Routledge, 1999, p. 1, http://site.ebrary.com/lib/dumlupinar/Doc?id=10054632&ppg=14.
2. Jean K. Chalaby (ed.), *Transnational Television Worldwide: Towards a New Media Order*, London: I.B. Tauris, 2005, p. 3, http://site.ebrary.com/lib/dumlupinar/Doc?id=10133061&ppg=11.
3. John Sinclair, 'International Television Channels in the Latin American Audiovisual Space', in Chalaby (ed.), *Transnational Television Worldwide*, pp. 4–5.
4. Walter Armbrust (ed.), *Mass Mediations: New Approaches to Popular Culture in the Middle East & Beyond*, Ewing, NJ: University of California Press, 2000, p. 37, http://site.ebrary.com/lib/dumlupinar/Doc?id=5003771&ppg=51.
5. Anthony Giddens, *The Consequences of Modernity*, Cambridge, UK: Polity Press, 1990.
6. Wojcieszak, Magdalena E., 'Al-Jazeera: A Challenge to Traditional Framing Research', *The International Communication Gazette* 69, 2007, pp. 115–28, http://search.ebscohost.com/login.aspx?direct=true&db=a9h&AN=24824142&site=ehost-live.
7. Naomi Sakr, 'Maverick or Model? Al-Jazeera's Impact on Arab Satellite Television', in Chalaby (ed.), *Transnational Television Worldwide*, pp. 66–91 (p. 70).
8. Louay Y. Bahry, 'The New Arab Media Phenomenon: Qatar's al-Jazeera', *Middle East Policy* 8 (2), June 2001, pp. 88–99, fn. 9, http://www.proquest.com/; accessed 2 January 2008.
9. Naomi Sakr, 'Maverick or Model?', p. 67.
10. Bahry, 'The New Arab Media Phenomenon', pp. 88–99.
11. Sakr, 'Maverick or Model?', p. 72.
12. Bahry, 'The New Arab Media Phenomenon', pp. 88–99.
13. Mariah Blake, 'FROM ALL SIDES', *Columbia Journalism Review* 43 (6), March 2005, pp. 16–18, http://www.proquest.com/; accessed 2 January 2008.
14. BG (*Boston Globe*), 'Middle East News Reports Are Not Welcomed By All', 5 February 2004, http://proquest.umi.com/pqdweb?index=0&did=543203571&SrchMode=1&sid=12&Fmt=3&VInst=PROD&VType=PQD&RQT=309&VName=PQD&TS=1180709693&clientId=46713.
15. Marc Lynch, 'Taking Arabs Seriously', *Foreign Affairs* 82, 2003, http://search.ebscohost.com/login.aspx?direct=true&db=a9h&AN=10580765&site=ehost-live.
16. Al-Jazeera Arabic, 2007a, http://www.aljazeera.net/NR/exeres/BE212265-7D56-420A-B99D-82D8624E6D41.htm.
17. Bahry, 'The New Arab Media Phenomenon', pp. 88–99.
18. Sakr, 'Maverick or Model?', p. 77.
19. Marc Lynch, 'Beyond the Arab Street: Iraq and the Arab Public Sphere', *Politics and Society* 31, 2003, p. 64.
20. AE (Al-Jazeera English), 'Programmes'; http://english.aljazeera.net/NR/exeres/3D7AB564-6F62-4899-B982-63B520D409F1.htm; accessed 18 October 2007.
21. AE (Al-Jazeera English), 'Programmes', http://english.aljazeera.net/NR/exeres/3D7AB564-6F62-4899-B982-63B520D409F1.htm; accessed 18 October 2007.

22 William A. Gamson, *Talking Politics*, Cambridge, UK: Cambridge University Press, 1992, pp. 3–7.
23 Entman, R., 'Framing: Toward Clarification of a Fractured Paradigm', *Journal of Communication* 43, 1993, p. 52.
24 Thomas E. Nelson and Rosalee A. Clawson, 'Media Framing of a Civil Liberties Conflict and Its Effect on Tolerance', *The American Political Science Review* 9, p. 7, http://www.proquest.com/; accessed 2 January 2008.
25 Stephen D. Tansey, *Politics: The Basics*, London and New York: Routledge, 1995, pp. 179–84.
26 Al-Jazeera English, 'Turkey PM to Address Nation', http://english.aljazeera.net/NR/exeres/FCEF7DF6–B180–4AFB-B3D5–553900A87C30.htm.
27 Al-Jazeera English, 'Erdogan Wants Polls to End Standoff', http://english.aljazeera.net/NR/exeres/BA5619F6–633E-4987–99D8–8868A1CA0AC1.htm.
28 Al-Jazeera English, 'Turkey Secularism Row Escalates', http://english.aljazeera.net/NR/exeres/975A9A02–802F-4CF4–AA91–6E128CD3A0B6.htm.
29 Al-Jazeera English, 'Turks Rally to Support Secularism', http://english.aljazeera.net/NR/exeres/9E015120–D8FF-4CEC-A6FA-A444B8309080.htm.
30 Al-Jazeera English, 'Turks March for Secularism', http://english.aljazeera.net/NR/exeres/archive7a42.html.
31 Al-Jazeera English, 'Second Pro-secular Demo in Turkey', http://english.aljazeera.net/NR/exeres/9E800CFC-AE37–4B67–BF03–B46EFDE1E0C0.htm.
32 Al-Jazeera English, 'Turks Hold Pro-secular Protest'.
33 Al-Jazeera English, 'Turkey Parties Urge Snap Election', http://english.aljazeera.net/NR/exeres/de89169c-80ac-4cc3–b6f3–85d01a03d6d0.htm.
34 Al-Jazeera English, 'Turks Rally in Izmir Despite Blast', http://english.aljazeera.net/NR/exeres/476B952C-8237–4629–9369–77DF4E1A7BC0.htm.
35 Al-Jazeera English, 'Turks March for Secularism'.
36 Al-Jazeera English, 'Turkey's Presidential Elections', http://english.aljazeera.net/NR/exeres/FBBDA4D7–DD4A-4C02–8904–756F184D1546.htm.
37 Al-Jazeera English, 'Turkey Faces New Election Timetable', http://english.aljazeera.net/NR/exeres/D5E8DB5D-3528–4BC8–B749–F501A994B99D.htm.
38 Al-Jazeera Arabic, http://www.aljazeera.net/NR/exeres/841B9B54–0E54–4461–8726–D2C9E19E339F.htm.
39 Al-Jazeera English, 'Erdoğan Wants Polls to End Standoff'.
40 Al-Jazeera English, 'Turks Rally to Support Secularism'.
41 Al-Jazeera English, 'Court Rules Turkish Poll Invalid', http://english.aljazeera.net/NR/exeres/E663047E-87CE-4FB6–8D97–DE31E6A6DD00.htm.
42 Al-Jazeera English, 'Erdoğan Wants Polls to End Standoff'.
43 Al-Jazeera English, 2007b, 'Turkey to Call General Election', http://english.aljazeera.net/NR/exeres/D2C78883–90A2–4068–B155–D8FE00DE5716.htm.
44 Al-Jazeera English, 'Erdoğan Wants Polls to End Standoff'.
45 Al-Jazeera Arabic, http://www.aljazeera.net/NR/exeres/FE94E606–E3AF-4EFC-A92F-265BDF25D025.htm.
46 Al-Jazeera Arabic, http://www.aljazeera.net/NR/exeres/2F409178–4DE5–4A7E-8047–45BB974EC8.htm.

47 Al-Jazeera Arabic, http://www.aljazeera.net/NR/exeres/1137081B-6F8B-4B4E-BB45-DAB1953DB2EF.htm.
48 Al-Jazeera Arabic, http://www.aljazeera.net/NR/exeres/3B383EA3-07D7-4618-BEE9-40393589738C.htm; Al-Jazeera Arabic, http://www.aljazeera.net/NR/exeres/1C4B0833-6819-4E1B-BE2D-13E63F189156.htm; Al-Jazeera Arabic, lttp://www.aljazeera.net/NR/exeres/B1C47B40-01B4-4052-BD2E-69C8AEFF75DE.htm. Al-Jazeera Arabic, http://www.aljazeera.net/NR/exeres/ EFD83092-0A4F-4448-8A5E-22025F863EEF.htm.
49 Al-Jazeera Arabic, Al-Jazeera website, http://www.aljazeera.net/NR/exeres/2A95FCB2-EE8D-4717-9F3E-F1ECF03F6B91.htm.
50 Al-Jazeera Arabic, http://www.aljazeera.net/NR/exeres/40529F66-2C2B-447A-AE0B-496C5A9D0475.htm.
51 Al-Jazeera Arabic, 2007k, http://www.aljazeera.net/NR/exeres/1C4B0833-6819-4E1B-BE2D-13E63F189156.htm.
52 Al-Jazeera Arabic, 2007g, http://www.aljazeera.net/NR/exeres/B6F03AE8-8B47-5DE-A507-48A3C804E010.htm.
53 Al-Jazeera Arabic, 2007g, http://www.aljazeera.net/NR/exeres/B6F03AE8-8B47-5DE-A507-48A3C804E010.htm.
54 Al-Jazeera Arabic, 2007p, http://www.aljazeera.net/NR/exeres/F3E86FC9-B836-4965-9C2E-B1BFBD3BEE0A.htm.
55 Al-Jazeera Arabic, 2007k, http://www.aljazeera.net/NR/exeres/1C4B0833-6819-4E1B-BE2D-13E63F189156.htm.
56 Al-Jazeera Arabic, 2007g, http://www.aljazeera.net/NR/exeres/B6F03AE8-8B47-5DE-A507-48A3C804E010.htm.
57 Al-Jazeera Arabic, 2007g, http://www.aljazeera.net/NR/exeres/B6F03AE8-8B47-5DE-A507-48A3C804E010.htm.
58 Al-Jazeera Arabic, 2007g, http://www.aljazeera.net/NR/exeres/B6F03AE8-8B47-5DE-A507-48A3C804E010.htm; Al-Jazeera Arabic, 2007i, http://www.aljazeera.net/NR/exeres/242AD656-21C6-450F-9F87-9CCB4717D4EE.htm; Al-Jazeera Arabic, 2007h, http://www.aljazeera.net/NR/exeres/841B9B54-0E54-4461-8726-D2C9E19E339F.htm.
59 Al-Jazeera Arabic, 2007i, http://www.aljazeera.net/NR/exeres/242AD656-21C6-450F-9F87-9CCB4717D4EE.htm.
60 Al-Jazeera Arabic, 2007k, http://www.aljazeera.net/NR/exeres/1C4B0833-6819-4E1B-BE2D-13E63F189156.htm.
61 Al-Jazeera Arabic, 2007j, http://www.aljazeera.net/NR/exeres/78CF75EB-94F7-4CD2-8904-A142168E38C4.htm.

2

Between Freedom and Coercion:
Inside Internet Implantation in the Middle East

Jon W. Anderson

Freedom and coercion have been prominent in thinking about the Internet in the Middle East, thinking that has focused primarily on the Internet as media and in relation to media politics in the region. As media, the Internet was widely hailed as an opportunity for democratic participation, or at least for more participation, in a region sorely wanting such opportunities. Many of those hopes have been dashed or abandoned, and blame has been attributed to the usual suspects, starting with the authoritarian state and culture.[1] It looked like another Middle Eastern 'exception', maybe even a deeper one, since other authoritarian states such as China saw phenomenal growth in both numbers and uses for the Internet.

The problem has typically been seen in terms of the low numbers of users, limited access, high costs and restraining authorities that can be documented dramatically in global comparisons by organizations whose own interests are in the spread of information technologies such as the International Telecommunications Union, the World Bank or the UNDP. But the image of low penetration, slow growth and limitation by and to elites derives at least as much from the framing of the Internet as media in the Middle East. As media, the Internet joins a long line of resources, from newspapers to broadcasting, hailed as emancipatory and framed in a cascading series of dichotomies: modern/traditional societies, open/closed cultures, developed/developing economies,[2] as well as newer ones about hierarchical versus flattened information regimes or centralized versus distributed communication, not to mention murkier metaphors of 'viral' communication or 'rhizomic' networks,[3] 'third' waves, and more that no longer require opposites to be stated, like Orientalism. Binaries are helpful for framing debate, but less useful for more grounded kinds of analysis, and discussion of the Internet generally as well as specifically in the Middle East can be a strong attractor of dichotomies that divert analysis into old channels more than towards new data.

Here, I would like to shift the ground to some new data on Internet implantation or implementations in the Middle East, which I have been studying with Michael C. Hudson at Georgetown University's Center for Contemporary Arab Studies. This work is different from the interest that Dale Eickelman and I framed in *New Media in the Muslim World*,[4] which examined the conjunctures of new media, new people, new interpretations and an emerging public sphere that some have found useful for developing additional material and others dismissed as utopian.[5] Our intention then was modestly to call attention to connections between publication and publics in various new media, and I think the model still stands for that purpose. But my interest here is less in that framing than in the culture and politics of Internet implantation.

Beyond advocacy on the Internet are Internet advocates, early adopters, and above all implementers in the Middle East. Here is where the habit of binaries tends to divert from what is there to what is not there. What is not there is well ventilated: numbers, access, affordability and the sort of information economy represented in Google, Wikipedia and subsequent developments down to blogging. In those terms, the world seems to have moved on, but in the Middle East the protean Internet that swept all before it and much into it seems to have proven more malleable by existing state structures and their capacities to reproduce themselves on the Internet. In Syria and Saudi Arabia, Internet installations parallel the phone system, but not in Jordan or Egypt, where struggles to free Internet service from phone companies had more success, at least partly by leveraging the goals of WTO compliance. Both Jordan and Egypt have been in the process of divesting their state telecommunications companies, so one story could be the freeing of entrepreneurial energies. Except most of this happened in the public sector, as indeed did Internet implantation in Syria and Saudi Arabia. These and other missing data in the usual stories of Internet implantation are what I want to bring into discussion.

Common storylines have the Internet invented for secure communication in the event of thermonuclear war, escaping from the clutches of the military-industrial complex into the public realm, only to be co-opted by corporate interests and commercialization. But the Internet was actually conceived by engineers for their own work, and assembled from existing technologies in multi-tasking, multi-user, multi-media and networked computing in a likeness of their own work habits and values.[6] Casting those values of flat hierarchies and self-administration as democratic attracted political attention in promoting the Internet as an information tool, which grew as a 'stack' of applications from email and file archives through the web portals and 'online communities' to the blogs and 'social networks' evident today. Each has its own engineers and engineering culture that share the idea of leveraging forces into 'social engineering', itself typically cast in the image of engineers' work habits and values.

Demographically, the Internet grew beyond the engineers who conceived it first to scientists, then throughout the research and academic world, to the professionals they trained and thence into the general public. These passages were marked in the USA by transfer to the National Science Foundation, opening to commercial exploitation, then World Wide Web interface and countless elaborations down to MySpace, Facebook, proliferating blogs that joined pre-existing portals and listservs as 'places' to find information, goods for sale and even friends, and also to project interests, identities and activities – from hobbies to hook-ups to terrorism. Its stages are marked technologically by mini-computer networking, the PC, and the Web, including the current incarnation called Web 2.0.[7] In the Muslim world, already a 'virtual community', these passages facilitated tech adepts who brought Islam online, 'officializers' who came to supply missing (to them) contexts, then 'modulators' who expanded those contexts to include practical, social and psychological contexts of contemporary Muslim life in the globalizing 'community' of bourgeois professionals.[8]

Shifting from the cultural space of Islam to the more political one of Middle East countries, a similar pattern begins with engineers bringing Internet technologies first to institutional sites of their own work.

Individual efforts brought these initially to universities, where the first Internet connections or component technologies were introduced; but more important were protected sites where expertise was gathered, developed and applied uniquely apart from both universities and line ministries with their pressures for bureaucratic orderliness, as well as from markets with their pressures for quarterly profits – that is, in institutionally public but intermediate spaces. What this means for Internet implantation is captured neither by the democratization nor by the co-optation theses but can be summarized as four points.

TABLE 2.1
Comparison of Internet development in Muslim (cultural) and Middle Eastern (political) space, with technological evolution from MIS-based to PC-based to web-based and sociological transitions from Creole Journeys through Elite Contention to today's Postmodern Nomadism.

Technology	Muslim Space (Culture)	Middle East Space (Politics)	Dominant Sociology
1970s–80s • Interactive computing • WAN, MIS • Listserv, newsgroups	**Tech Adepts** • Diaspora populations • Scientists and engineers • Put texts online	**Technocrats** • Administrative modernization • Governmental organizations	**Creole Journeys** • Internationalist • Public service • Modernization
Early to Mid-1990s • Personal computers give access • WWW for publication	**Activists** • Restore context • Official and oppositional 'content' providers	**Entrepreneurs** • IT niches • Development as globalization of markets	**Elite Contention** • Nationalist • Information managers • Globalization
Late 1990s • Interactive Web • Global networking	**Modulators** • Social/psychological contexts • 'New' *ulema*, modern professionals	**Software Developers** • Programmers and designers • Internal (regional) diaspora	**Postmodern Nomadism** • Transnational job circuits • 'Knowledge workers'

Source: adapted from Jon W. Anderson, 'Vers un théorie <<techno-pratique>> d'Internet dans le monde Arab', *Maghreb-Machrek*, 2004, no. 178, pp. 45–57.

First, both the Internet and its Middle Eastern contexts are complex and multipart. The Internet has always been a composite of computing technologies that grew by adding new uses and new users who then developed additional technologies. But this pattern is only partly replicated in the Middle East, where scientists and engineers trained in high-tech institutes brought back experience and expertise in Internet technologies and set about applying them. For the most part, they belong to the international spread of the Internet through institutions with better connections internationally than to their own societies.

Supplanting early individual efforts in engineering faculties, institutional efforts took various forms – the Royal Scientific Society in Jordan, a cabinet think tank in Egypt, a professional society of computing engineers in Syria, a telemedicine establishment in Saudi Arabia. Typically under patronage located a step away from the ruler, they were devoted to projects of modernizing 'soft' infrastructures (of administration) that paralleled efforts focused on hard infrastructures in the dominant Rostow paradigm of the day. Broadly speaking, their emphases were on computing for automation and networking as a way to spread computerization, and they initially sought Internet connections for that work, not as channels to their societies.

Pressure to open channels of communication to local societies came from the top, with a new generation of rulers who marked shifts from the predominant concern with national security of the independence generation to a greater concern with national welfare. Through international forums like Aspen and Davos, new-generation political leaders mingle with global information technology (IT) leaders and form a common reference group overlapping with a new technical elite eager to 'show how'. A MENA conference in 1995 that marked Jordan's return to favour in the Arab League displayed an Internet connection with much fanfare. It used facilities installed for telemedicine, which engineers employed to show Internet capabilities, and on which businesses subsequently attempted to piggy-back.

These limited disintermediations (such as flat structures and self-administration) imagined by engineers were seized upon by journalists and political pundits promoting the familiar and limitless liberationist 'Internetology' of open markets, open media, open government and open societies. Such ideas had more limited versions grounded in the expertise and goals of engineers and other applied scientists, who worked out of both the public limelight and apart from line responsibilities of ministries, on projects such as telemedicine, notably in Saudi Arabia and Jordan; the connecting of government agencies to suppliers, particularly in Syria and Egypt; telecom divestment and the developing of businesses in communication services, particularly in Jordan, Egypt and Saudi Arabia;

and the pushing of management information and decision support services 'outward' to other countries (from Egypt) and 'downward' to provincial administration (also Jordan).

Around the peripheries of these government-sector projects were other, more iconic ones: a pan-Arab Internet portal created by a doctor-turned-IT-journalist (and subsequently sold to a media magnate); Internet cafes added to fax services that serve refugees communicating with their home communities or around universities to capture students' leisure spending; a number of would-be international call-termination services; experiments in online journalism ranging from aggregation to original reporting through the Internet; a plethora of Islamic portals; and much more. The multi-part Internet 'fits' many potential contexts.

The second point to emerge is that these multiple settings lead to a lot of role-crossing, which has been analytically subsumed under an overemphasis on agency enhancement in Internet studies. In our comparative study of Internet implementations in Jordan, Syria, Saudi Arabia and Egypt we have seen a great deal of entrepreneurship, in the public sector more than in the private sector, which many engaged in IT there dismissed as limited to a 'business model of contacts and contracts'. This role-crossing starts at or near the top. Interests in the Internet and IT in general among rulers were ahead of institutionalized bureaucracies, including in the private sector (such as banks). This took institutional form in patronage located close to the ruler providing a protected site for engineers, who had won credibility on other projects, developing Internet installations and applications. In Jordan, for example, interest was led by the Royal Scientific Society (RSS), a government think tank under the active patronage of then Crown Prince Hassan, himself something of an international intellectual. In Syria, this role was played by the Syrian Computer Society (SCS) under Basil Al-Asad first and then Bashir Al-Asad, both sons of the president and one-time students of the core engineers who trained most of the early members of the SCS. The Egyptian equivalent was the Information and Decision Support Center (IDSC), a cabinet office think tank which took over initial Egyptian university connections to the Internet and promoted it for enhancing administration in both public (e-government, e-learning) and private (e-commerce) sectors. In Saudi Arabia, early connections by engineering faculties were rolled into a national and then regional scheme for telemedicine centred on the King Faisal Specialist Hospital and Research Center in Riyadh and subsequently linked to other Gulf countries.

These are the sites where the Internet started in an institutional sense and not just as individual efforts (or as raised consciousnesses). Each involved rolling up earlier individual efforts in engineering faculties of universities to make connections to the Internet. Each also leveraged a different expertise that moved beyond engineers' tools and problem-solving to public service. Moreover, apart from businesses and existing bureaucracies, they mark the rise of new technocrats.

Their institutional initiatives feature horizontal connections (an Internet standard) within government, across lines of vertical authority, although envisioning vertical connections to the public through electronic service delivery and even e-voting. They sought, and some actively recruited, allies in the business sector from financiers to potential developers of e-commerce in order to promote Internet acceptance and use, often for their own work in starting businesses themselves. They promoted the Internet in public sector projects that would give scope to their own work and bureaucratic advancement, quite the opposite of a brain-drain.

Third, this advent of the Internet through protected public sector institutes can be viewed as an institutional response to the Internet's lack of fit with existing industrial sectors. For the telecoms, media education, culture and security sectors, the Internet's protean character, which drew on a diverse set of actors and interests, meant that it did not truly fit into any of them. This was also the case with its engineering: was the Internet computing, networking, graphics, telecoms, a matter of programming? Engineers found ways to propagate Internet signals over alternatives, from microwaves to the SABRE system used for airline reservations to the public electricity grid. One told me about digging under streets to tap military fibre optics networks; others worked through colleagues or former students in the telecommunications companies to arrange connections to international circuits, if only to develop proofs of concept. Not only could almost anything migrate to the Internet, the Internet could piggy-back on almost any medium of signals propagation.

The result was that existing institutions could not contain the morphing capacities of the Internet – from its multiple underlying technologies in multi-user, multi-tasking computing, graphics and networking to its application layers from email and file archives to listservs and newsgroups, web portals and, lately, blogs – which form it as a 'stack' of applications, each with its own technologists and technological culture. New actors were constantly arriving. Competition to define, supply, channel and profit from Internet service arose in almost as many dimensions as it touched, crossing functional institutional boundaries and at once parochializing their interests and rendering many of their techniques anachronistic. In structural terms, it did not fit any institutional sector well enough or flow smoothly between them as Internet hype in the US had suggested in equating disintermediation with democratization.

So – and this is my fourth point – a series of new institutions were spawned in each country, straddling the public and private sectors, kinds of expertise, and a shift in development philosophy from modernization to globalization. They largely drew on public sector resources (from technical expertise to foreign aid), involved Internet champions in forming alliances and coalitions, and relied on a field of shifting patronage tied to generational succession within nations and internationally changing meanings of development. In Jordan, the RSS that served as an incubator for IT engineers' projects focused on administrative modernization was joined, and in patronage terms supplanted, by INT@J, an association of IT businesses but funded by a USAID project, with the goal of promoting IT not as a development tool but as a development sector. In Egypt, the IDSC (with United Nations Development Programme support) spawned the Regional Information Technology and Software Engineering Center (RITSEC) for spreading its model to other North African countries and a series of companies that took over successful demonstration projects, everything from providing government databases to a national Internet backbone. In Saudi Arabia, competition to provide Internet service beyond the telemedicine installation was resolved by placing the King Abdulazziz City of Science & Technology, the national centre for scientific research, between the state telecommunications company and both public (university) and private (commercial) service providers. In Syria, the SCS proposed a series of schemes to install, then to operate, then to design Internet service on top of the telephone system, which were successively whittled back to an Internet service provider (ISP) for its members, the first non-governmental one with a licence.

Each example reflects new configurations of constituencies that cross institutional boundaries, and a shift from IT as a development tool to IT as a development sector. At the same time that each new institution assembled or emerged as a network of interests, expertise, technological capacities, finance and regulation that converged on the Internet, the obverse occurred. Prominent members of the new technocratic elite passed into the formal government as agency heads, governors, ambassadors to Washington, London, Paris, and as ministers and agency heads. A former head of the Egyptian cabinet's IDSC became the first Minister for Communications & Information Technology, and was succeeded by another when he became Prime Minister. After Bashar Al-Asad succeeded his father as President of Syria, senior members of the Syrian Computer Society followed him into government as ministers, ambassadors, Governor of Damascus. The Jordanian ambassador to Washington, a computer engineer who had risen as a public sector technocrat, was succeeded by the first president of INT@J and himself went on to become Deputy Prime Minister.

This pattern is not limited to the 'hard' infrastructure of the Internet. It is pervasive in development of its 'soft' infrastructure as well. The company which created the first Arab portals was started by a medical school graduate, the region's first IT marketing research organization by a mechanical engineer-turned-journalist while working for a business communications firm. In Islamic cyberspace, companies formed to serve religious patrons, who bankrolled them to create Islamic websites. This pattern of role-shifting and boundary-crossing contributed to alliance-seeking and coalition-formation that is the story of Internet implantation.

The Internet in the Middle East began, as in the Internet's original home, as public sector projects, proceeded outward from engineers seeking allies, acquiring partners and moving from protected sites under high-level patronage into multi-player arenas. While versions of at least some engineering values and work habits passed into these arenas, the transferability of these values, and their universality, has been vastly overestimated. Focus on either their democratizing or co-optational virtues misses the more mundane processes of alliance-seeking and coalition formation both where the Internet originated and in its spread, or implementation, in the Middle East. In a study of Silicon Valley, Jan English-Lueck reported a pervasive sense of working not in the Valley or for companies located there but 'for the Valley'.[9] That is, IT workers exhibited a broad identification with IT itself. Something like that attitude seems to lodge in a cohort of public sector technocrats and their enablers in the Middle East who are no less IT enthusiasts than employees in Silicon Valley.

The paradox recedes, if it does not dissolve, by recasting the problem away from the dichotomies in which thinking about the Internet has been cast – from freedom versus coercion, with which I began, to traditional versus modern, open versus closed information regimes, hierarchical versus flat communication, colloquially Bell-heads versus Net-Heads or, almost metaphysically, West versus Rest. The conjunctions I've sketched here emerge instead as alliance-seeking and coalition-forming around the new technology that, because of the Internet's composite character, comes with a diverse set of actors even before they grow by acquiring more. What has been claimed to be boundary-busting in more developed economies and informational regimes has here sparked not just the rise of a new class of technocrats; it also led to institution-building as actors assemble and are assembled into networks around, not just through, multi-use technologies, a process that is invisible because of the overwhelming emphasis on agency enhancement in thinking about the Internet as media.[10]

The agency emphasis misses additional features of Internet regimes such as appeals to more 'universal' values over those of community, to expertise and to notions of multi-stakeholderism over representation. These are common features of networked communication, not only in commercial sectors but also in engineering ones as well as precisely where one would expect the Internet to work democracy-extending magic: the voluntaristic arenas of NGOs and transnational civil society.[11] For this sort of data, juxtaposing liberation by the Internet to co-optation by authoritarian states is not only stale. It also gets in the way of analyzing real Internet propagation, including the public sector as a core site of Internet enterprise and participation.

A near comparison to the public sector technocrats, rooted in engineering and working on administrative modernization from protected sites, is the overlapping but different world of the Islamic Internet. Each initially displays features of agency enhancement commonly associated with information technologies and manifest in new people deploying new media, pushing new interpretations into new or 'virtual' publics. Both the Islamic Internet and the Internet in the Middle East exceed the capacities of older institutions, particularly their capacities for boundary maintenance, and each displays the creation of new networks of allies.

Public sector technocrats working on the soft infrastructure of the Internet are joined by counterparts in the Muslim space that has come to include major sheikhs, individuals from many schools and most Islamic universities, as well as preachers like Yusuf al-Qaradawi or Amr Khaled. They join the engineers and other IT specialists who bring them online, creating a population of 'postmodern nomads' that circulates among regional centres in the Gulf, Cairo, the Levant and farther afield. A 'near overseas' of international agencies has been formed, passing in and out of 'revolving doors' between government and private sectors, non-profit as well as commercial enterprises. They include contemporary religious as well as technological adepts and a panoply of others from the arts and editorial professions. Theirs are networks articulated by alumni relations and agent chains (or flexible brokerage in skilled labour) that account for boundary-crossings better than the underlying sources of their projects.

The problem is that boundary-crossing is only half a story. Networks that are horizontally extended and vertically shallow adapt the political economy of flexible accumulation and its fragmented social capital to a cultural economy of expansive perspectives and opportunistic values that belie simple formulas of liberation through IT thwarted by old authoritarianisms. The peculiarity of the Internet is not agency enhancement but its home in the public sector, not a singular but a composite and constantly shifting character that belies agency enhancement. Some startling mobilities of people and ideas emerge within these parameters, however. Extensive negotiations, alliance-seeking and formation of coalitions around the new technology extend the public sector with new actors and attract additional actors to it. The cultural fragmentation that they bring comes with a post-representational register that is probably fundamental and surely misapprehended as liberation or as agency enhancement.

NOTES

1 A discussion that exists largely within political science, for which the initially optimistic version is Jon Alterman's *New Media, New Politics? From Satellite Television to the Internet in the Arab World*, Washington: Washington Institute for Near East Policy, 1998. Later, pessimistic assessments argued from a culturally based position – e.g., Mamoun Fandy, 'Information Technology, Trust and Social Change in the Arab World', *The Middle East Journal* 54, 2000, pp. 378–94 – or from global comparisons of policies and numbers – e.g., Shanthi Kalathil and Taylor C. Boas, *Open Networks, Closed Regimes: The Impact of the Internet on Authoritarian Rule*, Washington: Carnegie Endowment for International Peace, 2003.
2 Such as Daniel Lerner's *The Passing of Traditional Society: Modernizing the Middle East*, New York: The Free Press, 1958.
3 These conceptions of the Internet, which were held by the engineers who built it, and for which see Janet Abbate, *Inventing the Internet*, Cambridge, MA: The MIT Press, 1999, were widely translated into political terms by advocates such as Nicholas Negroponte, *Being Digital*, New York: Knopf, 1995.
4 Dale F. Eickelman and Jon W. Anderson, 'Redefining Muslim Publics', in Dale F. Eickelman and Jon W. Anderson (eds), *New Media in the Muslim World: The Emerging Public Sphere*, Bloomington: Indiana University Press, 2003 (1st edn 1999), pp. 1–18.
5 Yves Gonzales-Quijano, 'The Birth of a Media Ecosystem: Lebanon in the Internet Age', in Eickelman and Anderson (eds), *New Media in the Muslim World* (2nd edn), pp. 61–79; Marc Lynch, *Voices of the New Arab Public*, New York: Columbia University Press, 2006.
6 Janet Abbate, *Inventing the Internet*, op. cit.
7 See Milton L. Mueller, *Ruling the Root: Internet Governance and the Taming of Cyberspace*, Cambridge, MA: The MIT Press, 2002.
8 Jon W. Anderson, 'New Media, New Publics: Reconfiguring the Public Space of Islam', *Social Research* 70, 2003, pp. 887–906.
9 Jan A. English-Lueck, *Cultures@Silicon Valley*, Stanford, CA: Stanford University Press, 2002.
10 For an exploration of limitations of this view, see Emma C. Murphy, 'Agency and Space: The Political Impact of Information Technologies in the Gulf Arab States', *Third World Quarterly* 27, 2006, pp. 1059–83.
11 Jodi Dean, Jon W. Anderson and Geert Lovink, 'Introduction: The Post-democratic Governmentality of Networked Societies', in Dean, Anderson and Lovink (eds), *Reformatting Politics: Information Technology and Global Civil Society*, New York: Routledge, 2006, pp. xv–xxix.

3

The Milestone Metaphor: CNN and al-Jazeera Discourse on the Iraq War

Andreas Musolff and Abdel-mutaleb al-Zuweiri

Over the past four years, the war in Iraq has occupied a major part of news coverage in the international media. This particular war, as a part of the global 'War on Terror', has brought new challenges for politics, military, diplomacy and the media. Coverage of the war seems to dominate entire media organizations, and the enormous number of news reports offer researchers who are interested in such discourse rich data to be analyzed.

The language of media is a complex issue: strategies of language are deployed to influence the receiver towards a desired attitude or thought. According to Fabiszak,[1] media language has a 'significant influence on . . . public discourse'. She concludes that it 'is through the media that the social consensus on the conceptualization of social institutions is negotiated and achieved'.[2] One such strategy, which will be discussed in this chapter, is the use of metaphor.

Metaphors and their function in public discourse have received increased attention in recent years. In their classic book, *Metaphors We Live By*, Lakoff and Johnson acknowledged that metaphor plays a salient role in the structuring of discourse. They argued that 'many aspects of our experience cannot be clearly delineated in terms of the naturally emergent dimensions of our experience . . . this is typically the case for human emotions, abstract concepts, mental activity'.[3] Working from this basic assumption, a number of analyses based on Conceptual Metaphor Theory (CMT) have provided a substantial body of evidence for the importance of metaphor not only as a rhetorical feature but also as the cognitive basis for political debate.[4]

While some researchers[5] have explored the metaphors that emerged in the news prior to the start of military operations in the current Iraq war, this study analyses the news coverage of the conflict over the past four years. In order to compare what could be termed, broadly, Western and Arab perspectives, we have compiled a corpus of news reports from CNN and al-Jazeera International websites. In this study we focus on the metaphor of *passing a milestone* as a reference to political and military developments in this war, as in the following examples (italics in these and further examples have been added by the authors):

(1) Bringing Saddam Hussein to justice will not end the violence in Iraq, but it is an *important milestone* on Iraq's *course* to becoming a democracy.
(2) We now are passing another *important milestone* – the formation of a new government, a sovereign government of Iraq.
(3) A *grim milestone*: the number of deaths in the American-led coalition in Iraq surpassed 1,000 this week.

These few examples already give us an idea that the *milestone* metaphor is politically loaded to express a particular perspective on the progress of the war. In our study we want to investigate how – and how far – the *milestone* metaphor scenario frames the extension of this war over time and provides a basis for specific predictions and related evaluations concerning the outcome of the war.

Conceptual metaphors and metaphor scenarios

Conceptual Metaphor Theory (CMT) has been developed within the field of cognitive linguistics since it was first extensively explored by Lakoff and Johnson.[6] They put forward the essential CMT hypothesis that metaphor operates at the level of thinking. Metaphors link two conceptual domains, the *source* domain and the *target* domain. The source domain can be regarded as a set of entities, attributes, processes and relationships that are linked semantically and stored together in the mind. Such a domain is expressed in language through related words and expressions, which can be seen as organized in groups similar to those sometimes described as *lexical sets* or *lexical fields*. These words and expressions are sometimes called *linguistic metaphors* or *metaphorical expressions* to distinguish them from conceptual metaphors.

The target domain tends to be abstract, and takes its structure from the source domain, through the metaphorical link, or *conceptual metaphor*. Target domains are thus conceived of as having relationships between entities, attributes and processes that reflect those found in the source domain. For example, one of the conceptual metaphors that Lakoff and Johnson examined was 'love is a journey'. In this conceptual metaphor, the latter concept – i.e., 'journey' – invokes certain assumptions about concrete experiences and requires the reader and listener to apply them to the abstract concepts of 'love' in order to understand the sentence in which the conceptual metaphor is used. Consequently, CMT argues that few or even no abstract notions can be conceived of or talked about without metaphor: we understand them through the filter of source domain notions. The metaphorical filter always highlights certain aspects of the target domain and hides others at the same time. Thus metaphor involves a partial understanding of the target concept. This partial nature of metaphorical understanding and its conventionality are the crucial sources of the power and the possible danger of metaphor. Metaphors used in the mass media and in public policy can lead audiences into seeing things in the particular light that the politicians or media wish, while at the same time making it less likely that they will notice other facets of the topics under discussion.

Furthermore, particular sub-types of metaphors favour an even more specifically selective filtering. The American public's political attitudes, for instance, appear to be derived to a large extent from a 'common understanding of the nation as a family, with the government as parent'.[7] However, the worldviews of the two main political camps, i.e., liberal and conservative, are informed by two very different conceptual models of the family. While the conservative worldview is based on the *strict father* model, liberals build their worldview on the *nurturant parent* model. These models are applied metaphorically to the nation, forming two opposing versions of the *nation-as-family* metaphor. Liberals and conservatives thus use different cognitive–linguistic frameworks to assess moral issues. Consequently, studying social and political discourse can be done through analyzing the metaphors of that discourse. Therefore, we can apply the CMT notion of metaphor as a process of mapping from a *source domain* to *some target* to our initial set of examples:

(1*) Bringing Saddam Hussein to justice is *passing an important milestone*.

(2*) The formation of a new government is an *important milestone*.
(3*) The number of deaths in the American-led coalition in Iraq surpassed 1,000 is a *grim milestone*.

The conceptual mapping underlying examples (1*) to (3*) is the metaphor *significant events in the course of the war are milestones*, which links to a more general metaphor *a process over time* (e.g., the course of a war) *is movement along a path*, which has been researched extensively in cognitive linguistics as the 'event structure metaphor'.[8] At the specific level of the milestone metaphor, we can investigate different facets of its use in the Iraq war news by using the concept of *metaphor scenario*, which designates the 'set of assumptions made by competent members of a discourse community about "typical" aspects of a source situation; for example, its participants and their roles, the "dramatic" storylines and outcomes, and conventional evaluations'.[9] The scenario aspect is intended to capture the narrative and evaluative functions of metaphor, which are of special relevance in political discourse.

Metaphors of war
Discussing the metaphors that have been used by the American administration to justify the 1991 Gulf War, Lakoff[10] argued that two different sets of metaphorical definitions were employed, which led to two different scenarios. On the one hand, the *Self-Defence Scenario*, where Iraq was depicted as the aggressor and the United States and other developed nations as the presumptive victims of the aggression. The crime was the danger that Iraq could cause to economic health, and the American military action was thus presented as an act of heroic self-defence. The second scenario was the *Rescue Scenario*, where Kuwait was the victim, and raping (this word is used twice in the work, and though it obviously can be, and is, used with logical meaning fitting the desired context, because of the serious connotations of the word I would suggest using another) Kuwait was the crime: Iraq was again the aggressor, and the US came to the rescue of the victim. According to Lakoff, the American people accepted the latter scenario as the main moral justification for going to war. In the same vein, Lakoff also critically assessed metaphors such as *War is Business* and *War is Politics* in as far as they helped create public support for the war while hiding the true

justification and costs of the conflict. Iraq was often reduced to the figure of Saddam Hussein through the *State as (leader) Person* metonymy, and Saddam Hussein himself was depicted metaphorically as having invaded and raped Kuwait. Saddam was therefore a danger to his neighbours and the world and the United States was projected metaphorically as hero and rescuer.

In his analysis of the initial phase of the current Iraq war, Lakoff[11] has stated that many previous 'metaphorical ideas are back, but within a very different and more dangerous context'. Public support was activated by the US government through regular use of the term *War on Terror*. Lakoff outlines how the Bush administration once more played on the *nation-as-person* mapping to depict scenarios in which the United States was framed as both a hero and a victim. According to this frame, America must heroically take on the responsibility of disciplining the evil Iraqi ruler in order to stop him from using Weapons of Mass Destruction (WMDs) and at the same time rescue the Iraqi people from hardship and protect the interests of the civilized world. By drawing links between 9/11 and the war in Iraq, the United States is also pictured as the victim, acting in self-defence rather than as an imperial power. This shows that the two scenarios – i.e., the *Self-Defence* scenario and the *Rescue Scenario* – were working in parallel in the depiction of the current Iraq war.

In his 2004 analysis of metaphor use in the coverage of the Iraq war, Lule formulated the didactic objective that

> metaphors . . . can be identified and studied systematically, their implications made clear. And new metaphors – more thoughtful, encompassing, benign or instructive – can be offered for use. Such attention to the language of news can help inform reporting of war and guard against metaphors that kill.[12]

Lule focused on the banners that television networks use with their broadcasts, which consist of two or three words that identify and provide context for the text of the story. The wording of these banners was designed to motivate maximum interest and create maximum impact. Lule found that specific metaphorical phrases in *NBC Nightly News* worked to support the US administration's agenda:

> rather than investigate, analyze, or debate the rationale for war, the broadcast instead offered, through metaphor, a dramatization

of war unfolding. Accepting that the nation was on a *timetable*, dismissing inspections as the *games of Saddam*, giving voice to the frustration of the White House as it *lost patience* with the process, the broadcast then simply reported how the administration might *make its case* and *sell its plan*.[13]

Lule does not argue against the use of metaphors altogether. He found, like others, that metaphors are ubiquitous and form a necessary part of political discourse. Rather, he studied the implications of particular metaphors and offered alternatives that would highlight the importance of intellectual debate regarding contentious issues. For example, he suggested that the 'metaphor of a *claim* might have been a fruitful term to employ', because through it 'the Bush administration could have been understood as making particular *claims* about the regime of Saddam Hussein', thus inviting critical investigation and reflection of the claims. 'The metaphor of the *claim*, as opposed to, for example, *the games of Saddam*, would have suggested more questioning and reporting by the news media.'[14] His argument is that the broad journalistic goal should be encouraging dialogue and action without suggesting to the public only one particular choice of action.

In our study, we apply the methods of cognitive metaphor analysis and scenario analysis to war reports in CNN and al-Jazeera websites. The corpus sample of *milestone* metaphors includes 46 reports from CNN and 12 reports from al-Jazeera. The time period selected extended from 19 March 2003, the day bombs first fell on Baghdad, to 19 March 2007, the fourth anniversary of the American invasion of Iraq. For all texts, the specific source (*important, grim milestones*, etc.) and target domain aspects (Saddam Hussein's trial, formation of new government, death toll) were identified to establish the range of mappings and the main narrative/evaluative metaphor scenarios.

Data analysis
The *milestone* metaphor used by politicians, CNN and al-Jazeera, is part of a larger *movement/journey* scenario of the war. The language of movement pervades their reports. Some of this language comes directly from the Bush administration, the Iraqi politicians or the reporters of CNN and al-Jazeera. The *milestone* metaphor in particular and its collocations, i.e., *reach, pass, path, achieve*, etc., dominate the reporting of the war.

The Milestone Metaphor

In the reporting of both news networks, the Bush administration maps out a *path* that it is trying to *follow*. A path has *travellers, goals and final destinations. Progress* along the *path* is measured by the *milestones* that are reached. The *milestone* metaphor was used to validate how the government's plan was progressing towards a final set target. So the progression of the Iraq war is full of events. These events are the *milestones* that signify the completion of a major deliverable or a set of related deliverables. The following examples (continuing numerically from those given earlier) show the metaphoric system that connected the different news reports of the Iraq war in CNN and al-Jazeera over time:

(4) The adoption of a new law marks an *historic milestone* in the Iraqi people's long *journey* from tyranny and violence to liberty and peace (17 March 2004, al-Jazeera).
(5) US troop deaths reach *grim milestone* (13 April 2004, CNN).
(6) US death toll in Iraq passes 1,000: Democratic presidential candidate John Kerry called Tuesday's report a *'tragic milestone'*, and said the thoughts and prayers of all Americans are with those who have had family members killed in Iraq (8 September 2004, CNN).
(7) A trickle of Iraqis have begun voting in *milestone* elections designed to steer the country down the road of democracy (30 January 2005, CNN).
(8) Iraq's first freely elected parliament . . . marking *a major milestone* on the road to forming a new government (17 March 2005, al-Jazeera).
(9) 100th British soldier dies in Iraq: left-wing Member of Parliament George Galloway, one of those reading out the names, told CNN it was a *'melancholy milestone'* (1 February 2006, CNN).
(10) Nearly three months after an election hailed by the US as a *significant milestone* in Iraq's democratic process . . . (7 March 2006, al-Jazeera)
(11) Formal handover of the Iraqi military command structure under way: Casey said that 'today marks another *important milestone* in the relentless progress of the Iraqi armed forces' (8 September 2006, CNN).
(12) The fourth anniversary of the start of the Iraq war dominates the news now; it's an *obvious milestone* (19 March 2007, CNN).

While these examples obviously share the conceptual basis of the *path-movement-milestone* schema, they also exhibit crucial differences as regards the scenarios that provide the necessary context for their interpretation. Specifically, we propose the distinction of three different sub-scenarios that imply differing predictions concerning the outcome of the war.

The optimistic milestone scenario

Optimistic uses of the *milestone* metaphor are by far the most frequent in the corpus: they account for 50, out of 58 reports altogether, i.e., 86 per cent. Furthermore, the corpus shows that this scenario dominates reports of the Iraq war in the two news channels: both al-Jazeera and CNN repeatedly quote its use by politicians and other speakers, often without further comment. In this scenario, the users of the milestone metaphor – i.e., the US administration as well as sympathetic Iraqi politicians – portray the situation in Iraq and the war process as moving from one success to another, since a lot of *milestones* are being reached. This scenario is apparent in several news reports. President Bush stated that 'bringing Saddam Hussein to justice was an *important milestone* on Iraq's *course* to becoming a democracy'. However, in another situation, he regarded the nomination of 'new leaders of Iraq' as a *milestone* towards his victory in Iraq. Other American officials designated further milestones. According to the then Secretary of Defence, Donald Rumsfeld, 'the formation of a new government, a sovereign government of Iraq' could be considered a *milestone*. The Deputy White House Press Secretary, Scott Stanzel, declared that 'the court's decision' which upheld Hussein's death sentence, marked a *milestone* for the Iraqi people. From a military point of view, General George Casey, the US army's Chief of Staff, praised the fact that 'Iraq's air and naval forces and one of 10 Iraqi army divisions are under the operational command of the Iraq government' as a sign of having passed an *important milestone* 'in the relentless progress of the Iraqi armed forces'.

Iraqi politicians also made ample use of the *optimistic milestone-passed* scenario. On 14 July 2006, after 'Iraqi security forces assumed responsibility' for the relatively peaceful Muthanna province in southern Iraq, Mowaffak al-Rubaie, the Iraqi security advisor, called this event 'another *milestone* in our struggle to get to democracy, to freedom and to assuming full responsibility by the Iraqi security forces'. The Iraqi Finance Minister, Adil Abd al-Mahdi, interpreted the elections of 30 January 2005 as a *milestone* when he said that 'he feared the *milestone* polls could be marred by fraud'. It should be noted that with each use of the milestone metaphor in this scenario, the users supported the notion that the war plan was moving in the right direction. Both men hailed events in Iraq as milestones to provide the addressees with evidence of their successful mission. These milestones were characterized in different ways, such as *important, major, historical* and *significant*, to give them more credibility. The optimistic use of the milestone metaphor related to several targets in this war course, for instance, to Bush's *milestones* on 'Iraq's journey toward democracy' and 'toward our victory in Iraq', Casey's *important milestone* 'in the relentless progress of the Iraqi armed forces', and Stanzel's milestone regarding 'the Iraqi people's efforts to replace the rule of a tyrant with the rule of law'.

The repeated use of the milestone metaphor in the optimistic scenario has a hidden snag: if taken at face value, it puts in question the prominent 'mission accomplished' speech of President Bush on 1 May 2003.[15] The statement that a mission has been accomplished would normally imply that the final objective and goal of the journey in question had been reached successfully. However, if so many major milestones had to be passed after the 'mission accomplished' speech, one may well ask what goals have in fact been reached. And if the mission accomplished was, after all, not the final goal, what future goal do the post-May 2003 milestones lead to? The 'accomplishment' in May 2003 had been the relatively clearly defined end of the military conquest of Iraqi territory by the coalition troops, but what will be the difference between any supposed final goals, whether defined in military and/or political terms, or a further *milestone*? President Bush still used the metaphor nine times in his speech on 12 December 2005 but, intriguingly, he did not mention it once in his speech to the nation on a *change of course* in Iraq on 11 January 2007. Perhaps the *change of course* makes it difficult to find clearly identifiable *milestones*?

The milestone metaphor in the *progress*-oriented scenario offers an optimistic depiction of the progress of the Iraq war. It assumes that its users are accurate in their decisions and know the direction, the ultimate goals and the means of getting there. This metaphor was used to support the continuation and extension of this war effort and, judging by its frequency and popularity, it seems to have fulfilled that purpose, at least for a while.

The critical milestone scenario

The second type of scenario for the milestone metaphor directs attention towards the death toll for US and coalition forces in Iraq, an aspect that is hidden in the first scenario. It only appears in CNN reports and represents a small percentage of 11 per cent, or 5 out of 46 reports. Early on in the period studied, on 13 April 2004, CNN stated that US troop deaths reached a *'grim milestone'* when the number of US troops killed in Iraq reached 674. Three months later, a report in CNN said: 'In a *grim milestone*, the number of deaths in the American-led coalition in Iraq surpassed 1,000 this week' (example 5). On 8 September 2004, CNN quoted the Democratic presidential candidate, John Kerry, when he, too, called the US death toll of 1,000 a *'tragic milestone'*. In the same context, the left-wing MP, George Galloway, described the fact that the one hundredth British soldier had died in Iraq as a *'melancholy milestone'* (example 9). The metaphor of the *grim milestone* appeared again when 'U.S. troop deaths reached 3,000' on 31 December 2006.

The *grim, tragic* and *melancholy milestone* metaphors thematize the dark side of the Iraq war *path*. They show the other face of the Iraq war which is not only leading to *important* political *milestones*, but to *grim milestones* along the same *path*. Describing 1,000, 2,000 or 3,000 dead American or British army personnel respectively as a *'grim milestone'* makes the *progress* of the war look like failure. It raises at least implicitly the question of whether these sacrifices are justified and thus it could lead Americans and the coalition to lose their will to fight. Furthermore, the death toll of coalition forces, when viewed as *milestones*, represents an 'achievement' for the insurgents, which are portrayed as being still in the fight and having the capability to attack. The public may therefore find it difficult to believe the positive *path* version of the war story, as depicted in the first scenario. The true sign of success will be if American and coalition forces can go for an extended period of time without loss of life.

On the basis of this interpretation we can easily infer that the second scenario of the *milestone* metaphor will not be acceptable for those who subscribe to the first. There is corpus evidence for the conscious use of the two scenarios as competing interpretations of the war. In one report under the title '2000 Dead in Iraq Not a *milestone*', US Army Lt Col. Steve Boylan[16] was quoted as saying that the media should not consider the number some kind of *milestone*. Jeff Greenfield, a CNN senior analyst, in his report of 16 June 2006, called the 2,500 dead US forces in Iraq a 'grim *milestone*' and clarified the purpose of using this metaphor as being to change US public opinion. However, he stated at the end that: 'Nor did earlier "grim *milestones*" – the 1,000th death, the 2,000th death – produce any sharp change in U.S. public opinion.' Evidently, the reinterpretation of the *milestone* metaphor by way of its integration in a critical or pessimistic scenario of an ever-increasing death toll of coalition forces has so far not become a dominant or even equal competitor of the optimistic scenario.

The sceptical milestone scenario

Al-Jazeera reports in particular combine the use of the milestone metaphor with critical evaluations by way of re-contextualization. For example, although the fact that 'Iraq's first freely elected parliament in half a century began its opening session' was marked as 'a *major milestone* on the *road* to forming a new government' (example 8), this milestone was put into question by the further comment that 'a series of explosions targeted the gathering'. When the parliament's election was hailed by the US as 'a *significant milestone*' in 'Iraq's democratic process', al-Jazeera added the observation that 'the country's divided political factions are still fighting over the post of prime minister in the new government' (example 10). After Iraq's government took control of its armed forces, thus passing a '*crucial milestone*', according to US officials, this very milestone was located by al-Jazeera on 'the country's *difficult road* to independence'.

This scenario urges the public to think critically about the various milestones by linking them to other events on the same *path*, and it suggests that the war process in Iraq is not moving as smoothly as it is claimed in the first scenario. Implicitly, it invites the reader to reconsider the significance of the milestones that mark the *way* in Iraq. This scenario is only represented in three out of twelve al-Jazeera reports, with no attested occurrences in CNN. While its critical potential may be considered to be even stronger than the second scenario, which at least acknowledges the existence of milestones (albeit *grim, melancholy ones*), the limited corpus evidence seems to indicate that the sceptical scenario is restricted to the al-Jazeera view and that in terms of frequency of use it has not posed any major threat to the dominance of the first scenario so far.

Metaphors that extend the war

In May 2003, the war in Iraq was supposed to be finished, according to President Bush's 'mission accomplished' speech. Since then, however, the war has passed its fourth anniversary and its end is not in sight. As we have seen, CNN and al-Jazeera have metaphorically framed the war as a *movement* along a *path* towards a *goal*. The *progress* is measured by way of reference to *milestones*; the statement that specific *milestones* have been passed is part of a narrative-evaluative scenario. The statistically dominant use of *milestone* metaphor in the first scenario leads the public to think of the war process optimistically. The public repeatedly heard positive references to *passed milestones* from President Bush and his administration, who were in a better position to assign metaphors in a time of war than just about anyone else; so, many must have assumed that the war did indeed *move in the right direction*. Since this scenario also dominated the news coverage of the war in the global media, it will have had the greatest influence in shaping and guiding public perception. This scenario implies a prediction regarding a specific outcome of the war, i.e., victory for American and coalition forces, freedom and democracy for Iraqis.

The second and third scenarios contradict or undermine this optimistic view in different ways. While the second scenario does not deny the existence of *milestones* in the Iraq war process, the third scenario raises a fundamental question about their significance and, thus, the legitimacy of metaphorically speaking of *milestones* at all. The second scenario shifts the attention towards the awful face of the war, i.e., death and blood. It tries to convey to the public that these *important, crucial . . . milestones* are in fact *grim, tragic . . . milestones*. Furthermore, it says clearly that the 'achievements' in Iraq have been reached only over the dead bodies of American and coalition forces. The third scenario, on the other hand, shifts the attention towards thinking of the shortcomings of these *major, significant milestones,* by providing contextual information that contradicts the optimistic assessment, e.g., doubts about the ability to appoint the prime minister, further difficulties on the *road*, etc.

If the statistical evidence of scenario distribution in the corpus can be relied on, the first scenario is clearly the dominant one overall, with the second scenario providing the main alternative. The second scenario uncovers what the first scenario hides, i.e., the tragic consequence of this war for both Americans and Iraqis. When the *milestone* metaphor is integrated in a scenario that depicts the situation in Iraq as *moving* from one achievement to another, as in the first scenario, it hides the fact that thousands of Americans and Iraqis will be killed while *passing* or *reaching these milestones*. The first scenario therefore leaves no space for investigating, analyzing or debating the justification for lengthening the war. It offers instead a rationalization of continuing the war, at least from the US administration's perspective. If, however, politicians and international mainstream media were to give more prominence to the second scenario of '*grim, tragic milestones*' representing the number of deaths in the American-led coalition in Iraq, this might invite the public to reframe the debate over continuing the war. Instead of accepting uncritically the optimistic prediction of the outcome of the war as presupposed in the first scenario, the public might consider an alternative prediction of war outcome: a *journey into disaster*, i.e., a further increasing death toll. The third scenario, on the other hand, provides no clear prediction: it questions the first scenario and thus partially discredits the implied optimistic prediction, but indicates no definite alternative outcome.

Conclusions

This study applies CMT methods to analyze the rhetorical strategies used in the media, in particular al-Jazeera and CNN, in reporting the Iraq war news. The media is central in projecting the reality of war and often frames war with metaphors. Metaphoric language shapes thought, and because war is so pervasive in our metaphorical understanding, we need to be especially observant of the use of metaphors that configure war. The analysis of the *milestone* metaphor has shown three scenarios that depict the Iraq war as a *movement* along a specific *path* at significant points of the *journey*. The *positive* milestone scenario, which dominates the reports in both news channels, suggests a promising end to the war. This scenario can plausibly be connected to the public support of the war, whether explicit or tacit. The public, who received a huge amount of messages, all praising the supposed success in passing *important, crucial, major and significant milestones*, are being urged to think positively, not only of the progress of the war, but also of the results. This scenario would no longer be so powerful and influential if the *critical* milestone scenario with its emphasis on '*grim milestones*' was used more often in media reports. The *sceptical* scenario also could play an important role in changing public attitudes by undermining the default assumption of a positive outcome through contrasting the confident first scenario claims with non-fitting contextual information. So far, however, the predominant use of *milestone* metaphors in the optimistic scenario seems to have led the public to assume that the more *milestones* are achieved, the more accurate the US administration's policy decisions and predictions about future *progress* are. By reiterating this metaphor, the media are effectively extending the Iraq war *road* as long as there are *milestones* to be *passed*. According to Lakoff,[17] 'metaphors can kill'; this study proposes that not only can metaphors kill, but they can also extend the length of time that the killing continues.

NOTES

1 M. Fabiszak, *A Conceptual Metaphor Approach to War Discourse and its Implications*, Poznan: Adam Mickiewicz University Press, 2007, p. 13.
2 Ibid.
3 G. Lakoff and M. Johnson, *Metaphors We Live By*, Chicago and London: University of Chicago Press, 1980, p. 177.
4 J. Charteris-Black, *Politicians and Rhetoric: The Persuasive Power of Metaphor*, Basingstoke, Hampshire and New York: Palgrave Macmillan, 2005; G. Lakoff, *Moral Politics: How Liberals and Conservatives Think*, 2nd edn 2002, Chicago, IL: University of Chicago Press; R. Dirven *et al.*, *Language and Ideology* (Amsterdam studies in the theory and history of linguistic science, Series 3: Studies in the history of linguistics, vol. 204), Amsterdam: John Benjamins, 2001; A. Musolff, *Metaphor and Political Discourse: Analogical Reasoning in Debates about Europe*, Basingstoke, Hampshire: Palgrave Macmillan, 2004; J. Charteris-Black, *Corpus Approaches to Critical Metaphor Analysis*, Basingstoke, Hampshire, 2004: Palgrave Macmillan; Z. Kövecses, *Metaphor: A Practical Introduction*, New York and Oxford: Oxford University Press, 2002.
5 G. Lakoff, *Metaphor and War, Again*, 2003 (cited February 2008); available from: http://www.alternet.org/story/15414; J. Lule, 'War and its Metaphors: News Language and the Prelude to War in Iraq, *Journalism Studies* 5 (2), 2003, pp. 179–90.
6 G. Lakoff and M. Johnson, *Metaphors We Live By*, Chicago and London: University of Chicago Press, 1980.
7 G. Lakoff, *Moral Politics: How Liberals and Conservatives Think*, 2nd edn, Chicago, IL: University of Chicago Press, 2002, p. 35.
8 Z. Kövecses, *Metaphor: A Practical Introduction*, New York and Oxford: Oxford University Press, 2002, pp. 134–8. G. Lakoff and M. Johnson, *Philosophy in the Flesh: The Embodied Mind and Its Challenge to Western Thought*, New York: Basic Books, 1999, pp. 139–211.

9 A. Musolff, 'Metaphor Scenarios in Public Discourse', *Metaphor and Symbol* 21 (1), 2006, pp. 23–38 (p. 28).
10 G. Lakoff, *Metaphor and War: Metaphor in Politics – an Open Letter to the Internet from George Lakoff*, 1991 (cited 2008 February); available from: http://philosophy.uoregon.edu/metaphor/lakoff-l.htm.
11 G. Lakoff, *Metaphor and War, Again*, 2003 (cited 2008 February); available from: http://www.alternet.org/story/15414.
12 J. Lule, 'War and Its Metaphors: News Language and the Prelude to War in Iraq, 2003', *Journalism Studies* 5 (2), 2004, pp. 179–90.
13 Ibid., p. 187.
14 Ibid., p. 188.
15 G. W. Bush, *Mission Accomplished*, 2003 (cited February 2008); available from: http://www.cbsnews.com/stories/2003/05/01/iraq/main551946.shtml.
16 S. Boylan, *Military's Advice to Reporters: 2,000 Dead in Iraq 'Not a Milestone'*, 2005 (cited 2008 February); available from: http://www.editorandpublisher.com/eandp/news/article_display.jsp?vnu_content_id=1001351291.
17 G. Lakoff, *Metaphor and War, Again*, 2003 (cited 2008 February); available from: http://www.alternet.org/story/15414; G. Lakoff, *Metaphor and War: Metaphor in Politics – an Open Letter to the Internet from George Lakoff*, 1991 (cited 2008 February); available from: http://philosophy.uoregon.edu/metaphor/lakoff-l.htm.

4

News Media, Public Diplomacy and the 'War on Terror'

Saima Saeed

Introduction

> 'Truth can never be propagated by doing violence.'
> **M. K. Gandhi**

Terror sells! The twentieth century will go down in history for making wars a mass-mediated phenomenon. The way in which modern wars employ media, both before and during military operations, is indicative of how they are fought not just on geographically defined battlefields in the presence of those directly participating in the operations, but also symbolically. They are played out in the larger public arena of a hyper mediascape, as 'live' footage of the war zone compressing 'time-space distanciation' and enabling a worldwide audience to experience the 'reality out there'. Powerful news organizations exhibit their technological tour de force by airing events 'live' and as they unfold, extending the terror front into the home front.

So central have the media been in framing, mediating, administering and managing wars that scholars have expressed apprehension that increasingly 'foreign policy decision-making has become epiphenomenal to newsroom decision-making'. Many echo the conclusion that today 'news organizations determine which wars constitute news, who will cover them and for how long'.[1] At the same time it is also felt that this glut of images of terror does not necessarily make people more aware of human suffering but ends up trivializing it.

Mediated reality is not always 'real'. Representations are often made depending on which side of the fence one is on, much in the vein of President Bush's now infamous words, 'You're either with us or against us'. Media, instead of questioning this logic, become instrumental in furthering the 'just war' argument, resulting in Habermasian 'refeudalization of the public sphere'. From being the 'oxygen of democracy' to Thatcher's proclamation that publicity is the 'oxygen of terrorism', media's transformatory potential then becomes questionable.

Taking 9/11 as a case example, this chapter inquires into the contemporary use and impact of media for propaganda and public diplomacy. Since this one event changed forever the relationship between the Middle East and the West, it authenticated the hypothesis that modern wars are indeed media wars. Winning modern wars is as much dependent on carrying domestic and international public opinion as it is on defeating the enemy on the battlefield. Modern nation-state apparatuses stand to gain tremendously from controlling the media and shaping their output. It is worth recalling how in 1916 the Creel Commission had to 'manufacture consent' for the First World War, and how years later the 'Vietnam Syndrome' had to be cured. In waging the 'War on Terror' the US administration used four approaches towards utilizing communications and media as tools of war in a paradigmatic shift away from the way in which wars had previously been fought. Information is used not as an additional device of war but as one of its main weapons. I have identified these four areas of activity as follows: propaganda, information warfare, public diplomacy and news management.

All four are linked. Various permutations and combinations of the four uses have been applied – some long-term, others short-term – in an integrated and campaign-like manner, sometimes so closely linked with each other that it is hard to distinguish them from one another. The thin dividing line between *political news management* (especially of television and print media) and *propaganda* is often crossed. *Public diplomacy* stems from a more adept use of news media, this time in neutral and seemingly less political arenas like educational and cultural exchanges, to create a more favourable opinion of the United States in order to reduce suspicion and build credibility for its policies.

The diagram below illustrates how the four media devices created an enabling environment for the 'War on Terror' in what might become a defining feature of how wars will come to be fought and experienced in the twenty-first century.

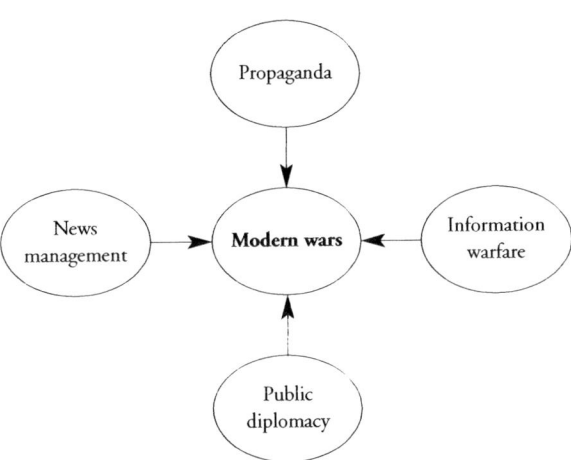

FIGURE 3.1
Media as instruments of war

The chapter is divided into two sections. In the first section I set out a conceptual framework within which to locate the relationship between media and democracy against the specific backdrop of how governments use media in war in order to control and manage public opinion both within their domestic public spheres as well as at the larger global levels. The second section studies the media reportage of 9/11 and the wars that followed, using two techniques; first through discourse analysis of some of George W. Bush's speeches in the run-up to the war in Iraq, and second, through a content analysis of newspaper and some television reports. The chapter seeks to identify patterns and practices of the Bush administrations in their use of information warfare, propaganda, news management and public diplomacy to win a consensus for its foreign policy. In so doing, the chapter further seeks to ascertain whether the news media have played an objective, transparent and fair role.

Engendering consent
Politics and journalism are two parallel processes, contiguous but separate, simultaneous but different. While the two rely on each other to varying degrees, both feeding from the other, the credibility of journalism as a profession rests on its independence from any political

control. Journalism that is controlled ceases to be a free, truthful and objective voice of the people – the very principles on which the 'fourth estate's' claim to power hinge. The history of the press in most countries has been not so much a history of its growth but of its struggle for freedom from the control of the state.

The much discussed work of the renowned American journalist and political scientist, Walter Lippmann, *Public Opinion* (originally published in 1922) is central to our understanding of news media and its relationship with society and truth. For Lippmann, 'news is not a mirror of social conditions, but the report of an aspect that has obtruded itself', something that he referred to as the 'pseudoenvironment', a fabrication of the real world. Only when social conditions take 'measurable shape' can the 'body of truth and the body of news coincide'. The press for Lippmann therefore cannot substitute institutions but 'like a beam of searchlight that moves restlessly about' it can bring issues from the darkness to light.[2]

Jürgen Habermas also saw the public exercising its will on matters that concern all, using 'undistorted communication'. Explaining his concept of the public sphere, Habermas wrote:

> By 'the public sphere' we mean first of all a realm of our social life in which something approaching public opinion can be formed. Access is guaranteed to all citizens. A portion of the public sphere comes into being in every conversation in which *private individuals assemble to form a public body* . . . In a large public body this kind of communication requires specific means of transmitting information and influencing those who receive it. Today newspapers and magazines, radio and television are the media of the public sphere.[3]

Elsewhere Habermas explains how public opinion is built over time in the public sphere which he likens to 'a network for communicating information and points of views (i.e., opinions expressing affirmative or negative attitudes); the streams of communication are, in the process, filtered and synthesized in such a way that they coalesce into bundles of topically specified *public* opinions'.[4] Habermas was concerned about the 'discursive level of opinion formation' in the political public sphere and its quality. Journalists are seen as important actors in this arena. They play a key role in selecting and deciding on programmes, controlling both demand for, and supply of, the news. As a result of organizational and hierarchical complexities, gatekeeping by editors, professionalization and routinization in the everyday functioning of newsrooms, 'effective channels of communication become more centralized' with time. For Habermas these 'selection processes become the source of a new sort of power'. Collective actors outside established political systems get fewer opportunities to influence the views and opinions presented in the mainstream media, which is why Habermas feared that the media themselves initiated a 'refeudalization of the public sphere'. He asserted that representations at both the political and semiotic level hinder critical debate and are the worst form of exploitation. Liberalism's ideals that all political will should be based on debate remain unfulfilled, and instead opinions are filtered through media industries whose disproportionate power and political hegemony distort the information that is presented to a hapless and unsuspecting citizenry.

How then might this media machine be brought to serve the modern state? Modern representative democracies, in order to maintain their legitimacy, power and control, have little option but to include citizens in their decision-making, to generate a consensus or a 'collective will' for their policies. For a democratic nation state fighting a war that involves a heavy loss of life, including the lives of its own soldiers, the media become an indispensable tool in generating the popular support that is necessary to legitimize its decisions.

However, when a state sells such policies to the public without giving its citizens an opportunity to formally vote, or even to hold informed debates around the issues, the citizens are reduced to the status of consumers, delivered to the state by the media. In this manner, the unsuspecting citizens forfeit their citizenship rights without recognition of their having done so because of the subtlety of the process. This leads to the atomization of the citizen and the fragmentation of reality. Corrupted by capitalist market mechanisms, the media ironically end up producing 'special forms of packaging news and views in a consciously integrative propaganda form'[5] in which community campaigns shape the public consciousness, its agenda and ultimately the public sphere. It is a form of propaganda which scholars term 'integration propaganda' and without which modern governments cannot survive. It is propagated not through stray pamphlets but in the main channels of communication – 'newspapers, television, movies, textbooks, political speeches produced by some of the most influential, powerful, and respected people in a society' – difficult to recognize because of its omnipresence.[6]

Propaganda wars

The uses and techniques of propaganda during the two world wars and throughout the Cold War era have been well documented and have clearly established the roles and virtues of the various media forms. German wartime propaganda used a variety of media, including leaflets and printed material, but most prominently the then recently-invented radio, which transmitted the speeches of Nazi leaders. For more than a decade the German Propaganda Minister, Paul Joseph Goebbels, was the brain behind the Nazi propaganda machine. In almost 6,800 pages of his writings (later recovered by the US authorities in Berlin) his philosophies of effective propaganda are laid out. Goebbels maintained that state propaganda should be planned and executed by one authority, which has to take the decisions as to when propaganda campaigns must be 'begun, augmented, diminished, and terminated'. The second principle that Goebbels advanced was that to evoke interest in the audience, propaganda must be transmitted through an 'attention-grabbing' communications medium. Goebbels personally preferred motion picture newsreels over radio because he thought that the images provided the 'proofs' for his propaganda contentions. Goebbels also created special 'news' stories to build around his propaganda. In a detailed study of Goebbels' methodologies of propaganda, Leonard Doob lists how 'funerals of prominent Nazis were made into newsworthy pageants; the same technique was applied to the French and Belgian victims of British air attacks. German and Nazi anniversaries were also celebrated routinely.'[7] A study of Nazi and Japanese radio propaganda found that the transcripts of foreign short-wave broadcasts were carefully constructed such that 'each item is a neat, tightly-packaged story, full of image words, dramatic, sharply-pointed, easy to remember'.[8] Charles Thomson, tracking the history of short-wave propaganda by the United States, established that the United States, despite being a relative late-starter, quickly caught up with its enemies. In 1941 only 13 international short-wave transmitters were available, mostly beaming programmes to Latin America. At the conclusion of the war, in 1945, the Office of War Information alone was using 36 transmitters in the continental United States and had installed 14 government-owned transmitters overseas. Even the captured transmitters in Europe and Asia were pressed into its service.[9]

Clearly, the power of the media in determining which events are delivered to the public and which are omitted, as well as how these events are encoded and conveyed, suggests an ordering of the world through media discourse. It implies the creation of meaning, as in the sense-making activity of the media. As Bernard Cohen remarked: 'The mass media may not be successful in telling us what to think, but they are stunningly successful in telling us what to think about.'[10] Or as Pierre Bourdieu puts it, the very fact of reporting or putting on record 'always implies a social construction of reality that can mobilize (or demobilize) individuals or groups'. For him the greatest stake today 'in local as well as global political struggle is the (media's) capacity to impose a way of seeing the world, of making people wear glasses that force them to see the world divided up in certain ways . . . Television plays a determining role in all such struggles today.'

A generally repeated theme in writings like these refers to our experience in today's world as being largely 'mediated' by the media itself. Denis McQuail suggests that control over the mass media consequently offers definite advantages. First, the media helps attract and direct attention to problems. Second, the mass media can help confer status and legitimacy. Third, it can also be a channel for persuasion and mobilization. And finally, the media can help 'bring certain kinds of publics into being and help maintain them'.[11] Maxwell McCombs and Donald Shaw dealt with the 'agenda-setting' function of the press in depth in their seminal work in the 1960s and 70s. By 'agenda-setting' McCombs and Shaw meant the ability of the media to 'mentally order and organize our world for us', which gives it sweeping political powers. Their hypothesis was that the 'mass media set the agenda for each political campaign, influencing the salience of attitudes towards the political issues'.[12]

Neo-Marxists go further still. Building on Antonio Gramsci's concept of hegemony, they argue that news content routinely supports the dominant ideology, hegemony referring to the processes by which the dominant ruling classes influence and shape popular consent through the production and diffusion of meanings. As Raymond Williams has argued, 'hegemony has continually to be renewed, recreated, defended, and modified'.[13]

Arguably, this is nowhere more apparent than in the United States itself. Peter Dahlgren has shown how the powerful American media lends support to American foreign policy by creating particular images of its opponents. This is done through news narratives that position violence in the foreground, while the social and political factors which it expresses recede to the background. Ideologically, violence in these societies is shown to be a consequence of their internal instability. The media create and support the 'motif of disorder with sub motifs of violence/unrest, subversion and combat' by deliberately omitting any analysis of the Third World's historical and social causes of conflicts. And, as Dahlgren says:

> the systematic coercion and terror that many of these governments use to maintain their power is usually not termed as 'violence' . . . What develops is a case of 'them' and 'us', 'they', the people of the Third World and 'we' the industrialized West typified by order and stability, a higher form of civilization.[14]

Noam Chomsky and Edward Herman, through their substantial body of political writings, likewise contribute to this understanding. They analyze what they term the 'propaganda model' of the US media in their book, *Manufacturing Consent*. They argue that since media news outlets are now run by large corporations, they work under the same economic and political pressures as any other big businesses. The elite domination of the media and the marginalization of dissidents results from the operation of what they identify as news 'filters', which are the essential ingredients of their propaganda model. These news filters are as follows:

> (1) the size, concentrated ownership, owner wealth, and profit orientation of the dominant mass-media firms; (2) advertising as the primary income source of the mass media; (3) the reliance of the media on information provided by government, business, and 'experts' funded and approved by these primary sources and agents of power; (4) 'flak' as a means of disciplining the media; and (5) 'anticommunism' as a national religion and control mechanism. These elements interact with and reinforce one another. The raw material of news must pass through successive filters, leaving only the cleansed residue fit to print. They fix the premises of discourse and interpretation, and the definition of what is newsworthy in the first place, and they explain the basis and operations of what amount to propaganda campaigns.[15]

Thus we are left with the conclusion that what is most important is not how much power the media has but rather who controls the media and to what ends?

Information warfare

Nowhere is this more true than in the conduct of modern warfare. The 'industrialization of war' was a defining feature of the twentieth century. Technologies which allowed for the mass production of weapons and enabled the rapid movement of troops played a large part in shaping the two world wars and the geopolitical configurations that followed. On the communications front, the telegraph redefined the speed with which messages were sent to the troops on the battlefield, and further developments in telecommunications and information technology helped in the subsequent advancement of the conduct of warfare.

So close became the association between communication technologies and the military that the field of electronics matured only after requirements in war forced advances in the field of radar, fire control and, later, the development of the first computer. The Electronic Numerical Integrator and Calculator (ENIAC) developed by the University of Pennsylvania in 1943 was financed and sponsored by the army. Even the first communication satellite system was a result of efforts by the military, and the Pentagon was behind the discovery of COBOL (Common Business Oriented Language).[16]

The coordination of the means of warfare with technological developments in communication in a very real sense changed the way modern wars came to be conceived and fought, with far-reaching implications. For Giddens, for example, the *control of information*, along with *centralized control over the means of* violence, is the key to the organization of modern state systems.[17]

In a paradigmatic shift, wars have in practice become as much activities of Information Operations (IO) as military events. Information comprises the second arsenal in the armoury of modern warfare, victory lying with the side that has superior technology for controlling and processing information. If the 1991 Gulf War was the first television war in terms of being broadcast live, the wars fought since 2000 have become 'e-driven', relying heavily on computer simulations, global surveillance and media manipulation, representation and framing. For Frank Webster, 'information warfare in the era of globalization' is replacing the 'industrial warfare' that was fought in the twentieth century. In the case of the United States, even a new doctrine of war has been engineered, so-called network-centric warfare (NCW), also termed network-centric operations (NCO). Pioneered by the United States

Department of Defence, NCW/NCO seeks to translate an information advantage, enabled in part by information technology, into a competitive advantage in war, by employing advanced networking of well-informed geographically dispersed forces. 'NCW translates information superiority into combat power by effectively linking knowledgeable entities in the battlespace' across timezones.[18]

This warfare, guided by computer-aided operations, achieves a unique compression of time and space, serving to dehumanize war, making it virtual, televisual and a fit subject for transmission and consumption. 'Battlespaces' replace traditional 'battlefields' to convey a sense that 'the mission environment or competitive space encompasses far more than a contiguous physical place'.[19] Warfare becomes much more than the process of physical engagement; it becomes a 'total war', where sides battle to engage the hearts and minds of entire populations and today's military commanders stand to gain more than ever before from controlling the media and shaping their output.[20]

The concept of psychological war is not new, of course: it gained usage after the First World War and primarily employs propaganda for external control and 'pacification' at the domestic level. Psychological warfare is a communication that impacts on the sense, feelings and thinking patterns of an entire population. Psychological wars therefore involve what Armand Mattelart calls the 'systematization of the population's political indoctrination' so that it can be moulded as required. Antony Giddens eloquently argues that internal pacification is made possible because of a 'heightened administrative unity', which in turn helps 'police' civil disturbances. The whole system is based on surveillance whereby the state can keep a watch over the activities of its population.[21]

The ideology of national security and the development of public diplomacy

In the United States, headway has been made in this direction through the linking of this notion of total war with the policies of national security. The doctrine of national security has provided a justification for war, whether political, psychological or social, in the name of maintaining the unity, integrity and security of the nation. This doctrine found its legal manifestation in the National Security Act of 1947, which allowed for the setting up of wartime institutions and 'made the war priorities of the period also peace-time priorities'. It further provided for 'an integration of the foreign policy with the national policy, also linking security with notions of development.[22] From this doctrine were born the Central Intelligence Agency (CIA) and the National Security Council, two bodies that have extraordinary executive control over all matters of defence and foreign policy. For Mattelart, 'the very existence of the CIA introduced and sanctified secret activities and surveillance as standard State policies'.[23] Under the pretext of national security even propaganda began to be legitimized. It also allowed the government to crush what it calls 'subversive propaganda', which it deems to be antithetical to its interest. It is perhaps useful at this point to recapitulate one of the widely used definitions of propaganda as a 'deliberate and systematic attempt to shape perceptions, manipulate cognitions, and direct behavior to achieve a response that furthers the desired intent of the propagandist'.[24]

Developments in both communications and international governance changed the dynamics of this policy-making. With the intensification of globalization, both in reach and in influence, global governance has moved away from the long-held traditional model of states working in a limited number of organizations to dictate administrative rules towards a more fluid and heterogeneous policy architecture in which states have to work closely, negotiating and competing with other actors both within and beyond their sovereign boundaries. In this environment the state, as a master organizer of consensus, needs to direct its propaganda not just within the confines of its domestic public sphere but also at the global public in order to win allies and support from the international community. In this it uses diplomacy and public relation techniques, the third approach to using media in war. In the period following the Cold War, public diplomacy became so important that governments could not afford to overlook it.

In the 'battle for hearts and minds', image-making has subsequently become an integral part of foreign policy. Yet American foreign policy-makers have not entirely learned this lesson. The period following the launch of the war in Iraq saw strong anti-American sentiments in most of the Asian and Middle Eastern counties. Leonard, in his detailed study of media and diplomacy, asserted that in the post-9/11 era 'public diplomacy has not failed to deliver information [but] rather it has failed to deliver information convincingly'. He shows how the tone of many messages by the US was 'declamatory without any apparent intent to engage in dialogue or listen'. Leonard is particularly critical of the way the US government resorted to crude psychological operations such as dropping leaflet bombs, because its text was very 'forensic'. For him these sorts of messages become enmeshed in a 'battleground of "your information versus my information".[25]

Heads of states build public support for policies by regularly speaking directly to the citizens and generating positive news content through the press which, if done well, can provide the governments with what Samuel Kernell declares to be 'near-monopoly control' over policy and news agendas.[26] Arguably, this is precisely what the Bush administration did to make the case for what it called a 'just war'. Each time President Bush decided on any fresh intervention he first laid the grounds for it by a series of highly published media interventions. Central to the whole debate about how the visual news media create meanings and make us see events in a certain way is Gitlin's and later Gamson and Modigliani's analysis of 'media frames' or interpretative patterns. For Gitlin 'media frames' are 'persistent patterns of cognition interpretation, and presentation, of selection, emphasis and exclusion by which symbolic-handlers routinely organize discourse'.[27]

In the next section I analyze the language, timing and rhetoric employed in three speeches by President George W. Bush made in three consecutive years: 2001, 2002 and 2003.[28] A discourse analysis of his speeches maps the following four contexts – first, that of the president's attempt at justifying the war; second, the creation of the image of the enemy; third, his doctrine of the 'rogue states' and positioning of the home nation US as the protector against these terrorists; and lastly, a call to the international community to join this 'War on Terror' as the morally correct thing to do.

Bush's 'call to arms': the 'just war' argument

On 20 September 2001, Bush gave his State of the Union address to the joint session of the Congress and the American people. The speech was delivered in anticipation of the war on Afghanistan, titled *Operation Enduring Freedom*, which began in the same year. The name of this military operation or war was carefully chosen: as with the subsequent war in Iraq, titled *Operation Iraqi Freedom*, its name ended with the word freedom, which lent it a moral sanctity. G. W. Bush built his argument thus: 'On September the 11th, enemies of freedom committed an act of war against our country.' He expanded on the terrorist action: 'The terrorists' directive commands them to kill Christians and Jews, to kill all Americans, and make no distinction among military and civilians, including women and children.' He described the terrorists as 'heirs of all the murderous ideologies of the 20th century . . . they follow in the path of fascism, and Nazism, and totalitarianism'. Finally, he divided the world into two: the civilized world and the terrorists. Bush said: 'The civilized world is rallying to America's side.' He ended with a prayer. 'Fellow citizens, we'll meet violence with patient justice . . . assured of the rightness of our cause, and confident of the victories to come.'

The State of the Union address given on 29 January 2002 is equally interesting. Stating the progress made in Afghanistan, Bush said: 'The last time we met in this chamber, the mothers and daughters of Afghanistan were captives in their own homes, forbidden from working or going to school. Today women are free, and are part of Afghanistan's new government.' He went on to pre-empt his upcoming aggression against Iraq. He named three nations on his hit list that had to be chastized as they formed what he called an *axis of evil*:

> North Korea is a regime arming with missiles and weapons of mass destruction, while starving its citizens. Iran aggressively pursues these weapons and exports terror, while an unelected few repress the Iranian people's hope for freedom. Iraq continues to flaunt its hostility toward America and to support terror. The Iraqi regime has plotted to develop anthrax, and nerve gas, and nuclear weapons for over a decade. This is a regime that has already used poison gas to murder thousands of its own citizens . . . States like these, and their terrorist allies, constitute an axis of evil, arming to threaten the peace of the world . . .

Then he resolutely pronounced to the world: 'And all nations should know: America will do what is necessary to ensure our nation's security.' The speech made it clear that nations must either ally with the US and be a part of the civilized world, or be identified with the 'axis of evil', with dire consequences.

Exactly a year later, on 28 January 2003, the State of the Union address showed a change of emphasis. This speech showed Bush's complete distrust of the Iraqi president: 'The dictator of Iraq is not disarming. To the contrary; he is deceiving.' President Bush continued by giving details of the weapons that Saddam possessed, citing the following figures:

> The United Nations concluded in 1999 that Saddam Hussein had biological weapons sufficient to produce over 25,000 liters of anthrax . . . enough doses to kill several million people. He hasn't accounted for that material. He's given no evidence that he has destroyed it. Our intelligence officials estimate that Saddam Hussein had the materials to produce as much as 500 tons of sarin, mustard and VX nerve agent.

In hindsight this demonstrates the Pentagon's capacity for 'spin', as it was brought to light in later years that Saddam Hussein did not possess WMDs.

Then in a mysterious twist in his speech and as an outstanding example of political spin, President Bush strangely connected 9/11 to Saddam Hussein in a dramatic and provocative manner. In his words:

> Imagine those 19 hijackers with other weapons and other plans . . . this time armed by Saddam Hussein. It would take one vial, one canister, one crate slipped into this country to bring a day of horror like none we have ever known. We will do everything in our power to make sure that that day never comes.

It is worth taking a quick look at some public opinion polls which point to the subsequently skewed understanding of the reasons for 'War on Terror'. In a *New York Times*/CBS News poll, conducted over the weeks leading up to the invasion in Iraq, 45 per cent of respondents said that Saddam Hussein was directly involved in the 9/11 attacks. The *Washington Post* poll reported that nearly 7 in 10 respondents thought that Hussein was involved in the attack.

The news 'spin' post-9/11

This brings us to the fourth media weapon in modern wars: that of political news management. One has only to count the number of times between 2001 and 2007 that President Bush used the radio to address the nation on the issue of war to realize the kind of importance that the White House gave to mass media in generating a mandate for war. The first of these radio messages began on 29 September 2001, on the topic *Progress Made in the War on Terrorism*. Thereafter, in just three months (from October 2001 to December 2001) President Bush addressed the issue on radio a further five times. It is worth asking just why a president should feel the need to go public with such issues as often as two to three times a month through the media.

TABLE 3.1
Going public with war

Year of the radio address	Number of radio addresses on the issues of war on Iraq/the Middle East/ Saddam Hussein
2001	6
2002	11
2003	22
2004	17
2005	15
2006	14
2007 (up to September 2007)	10

Source: 'Radio Addresses of President George W. Bush', The White House website, Radio Address archives; http://www.whitehouse.gov/news/releases/2001/09/20010929.html (accessed August–September 2007).

TABLE 3.2
Propaganda and radio

Date of the radio address	Titles of the radio address/number of such addresses on the issue of war
29 September 2001	Progress Made in the War on Terrorism
27 October 2001	Legislation in War on Terrorism
22 December 2001	Economy and Terrorism
16 March 2002	Children of Afghanistan
6 April 2002	Middle East
20 April 2002	Middle East
8 June 2002	Terrorism
14 September 2002	Saddam Hussein
21 September 2002	Department of Homeland Security
27 September 2003	Iraq
1 November 2003	Iraq
17 April, 24 July, 27 August, 11 September 2004	4 out of 17 were titled '9/11 Commission'
2 April 2005	WMD Commission Report
18 March 2006	Operation Iraqi Freedom: Three Years Later
23 September 2006	Peace in Middle East and Democracy in Iraq
January–September 2007	Four out of 10 such addresses were titled 'The Way Forward in Iraq'

Source: Radio address of President George W. Bush, The White House website, Radio Address archives; http://www.whitehouse.gov/news/releases/2001/09/20010929.html (accessed August–September 2007).

Television wars: visuals don't lie

Radio is still a tame, harmless medium by today's standards. It relies on words alone to convey the impact of events. By contrast, the power of live television was unleashed during the Gulf War through instant narrativization and instantaneous visibility. The fetish of news networks for war stories is evident from the fact that, years later, even as late as the sixth anniversary of 9/11 in 2007, both the BBC and CNN had Iraq 'report card' as their top story. Arguably, this is a continuation of the trend set by coverage of the events of 9/11 itself.

So tiring and voluminous has been the ritualized representation of 9/11 in the media that there have been reports of people complaining about '9/11 fatigue'. In March 2004, a CNN report titled 'Some 9/11 families want Bush ads yanked', revealed that some relatives of those killed on 9/11 had asked President Bush to pull his new campaign commercials off the air immediately, saying they were outraged over their use of imagery from the 2001 terrorist attacks.[29] Bob McIlvaine, who lost his 26-year-old son in the World Trade Center attacks, said: 'It upsets me tremendously that Bobby, my son, could be used as a political pawn to be manipulated and at times abused – it truly makes me sick.'

Critics suggest that television reduces the realities of war and merely makes a spectacle out of it. The much-criticized phrase 'Shock and Awe' used by a veteran war correspondent to describe the Baghdad night sky as US and British forces rained close to 1,500 bombs and missiles down on the ancient Iraqi capital exemplified how television news sadly ended up trivializing a disastrous war into a Reality TV drama for viewers. On 21 March 2003, as the whole world watched this television spectacle of war, reporters both in Baghdad and the US sprung into action. 'The sky is lit up, Tom!' shouted veteran war correspondent Peter Arnett to NBC News anchor Tom Brokaw. 'Just like out of an action movie, but this is real, this is real; this is shock and awe, Tom!' Brokaw took his cue. 'The overture is over', he replied. 'This is the main piece.'[30]

The well-dressed anchors sit in their television studios thousands of miles away from the atrocities of aerial attacks while raw footage is rolled out to establish the technological prowess of each channel as the first to 'break' the story. This was best illustrated in the live phone call that took place between a CNN morning anchor and a victim, Mellisa Doi, who was caught on the 86th floor of one of the Word Trade Center towers on the morning of 9/11. Even in such a situation, all that the news anchor kept repeating to Mellisa was 'calm down, calm down', subsequently repeatedly insisting that Doi answer her question as to whether she could see only smoke or whether there was fire as well. Amidst the chaos of frenzied shouting in the background and screams for help, Mellisa Doi died even as the phone call remained live.

In their coverage of the Iraq war, many news organizations incorporated red, white and blue logos into their visual promotions. Journalists sported patriotic lapel flags, studio discussion happened against plasma backgrounds of 9/11 footage. For Baudrillard, the fallout from this relentless visibility is an 'obscenity of the visible, of the all-too-visible . . . of what no longer has any secret, of what dissolves completely in information and communication'.[31] The reduction of current events to what Bourdieu calls a 'litany of events with no beginning and no real end' and its resultant effect of depoliticization – that is, the public's disenchantment with political events – is an opinion echoed by many.[32] The Abu Ghraib prison photos and the controversies that came to surround them further illustrate how the media indulge in the visual spectacle and lead to fragmentation and hatred amongst people.

Some key questions in need of urgent answers stand out. Has the media through this kind of coverage helped reinforce stereotypes leading to a distorted (and even Islamaphobic) understanding of the wars? Will the media, as the 'hypermarkets of terror videos' and 'producers of shock and awe therapy', be able to regulate themselves? Where must we draw the line when showing images of extreme violence?

Media muzzled

The role of journalists in reporting conflicts has not received the kind of scholarly attention that it deserves. It was Bernard Cohen who was the first to separate the 'neutral' role of a journalist from his 'participant' role. The former is based on a journalist's autonomy as a political actor, the second on his positioning as a political actor. In the current era, and as the 'War on Terror' demonstrates, the tradition of the 'watchdog journalist', the neutral reporter of events, is fast diminishing as the political role advances. Thomas Patterson made a five-country survey of 1,300 journalists, which concluded that a prime reason for the above decline is that journalists are expected to perform many roles at the same time: 'watchdog, messenger, reporter, analyst, advocate, broker'.[33] The problem is that these roles are not fully compatible. In focusing on one, the journalist inevitably diminishes his or her ability to do justice to the others.

This brings us to questions about standards of 'objectivity' in news reporting. Truth, relevance, balanced reporting and neutral presentation amounting to factuality and impartiality in reporting have been seen as hallmarks of objective reporting.[34] In its 'War on Terror', however, the US muzzled the media in two crucial ways. First, by 'embedding' reporters; second, by allegedly bombing al-Jazeera, an important channel in the Arab world with a considerable audience in the region, thus threatening news diversity. Because of the above, and linked to these, the global media failed to ask hard-hitting questions, ultimately becoming a mouthpiece of the US. In an interesting study, indicative of how governments manage news, scholars like Grossman and Kumar have traced the institutional development within the White House of the Office of the Press Secretary to handle the president's relations with reporters. As reporters are dependent upon the White House for news, the administration can shape the coverage the press receives by restricting the flow of information. Journalists often go by what Lance Bennett called 'indexing' by government sources, which all but identify the key areas they consider need to be flagged concerning any government issue or statement.[35]

Yoram Peri explains further how the war reporter does not have the freedom to write what he or she wants.[36] Unlike in other fields, information in the realm of national security is held as a virtual monopoly. When it comes to national security, the sources of information are few and access to them is controlled. James Compton also suggests a nexus between power elites, the military and the media. As Compton says:

> The goal was to produce dramatic and sympathetic stories about the troops. Their solution was to attach, or 'embed', more than 600 reporters with specific military units. These reporters travelled 24 hours a day under the protection of the same soldiers they were supposed to write stories about.

Commentators added that 'those embedded' could only see what military personnel allowed them to see.[37]

Of course unprecedented censorship in the name of national security is nothing new, but the bombing of the 'enemy media' reveals the ideological discourse of completely disallowing any alternative point of view, in this case the media from the Arab World. On 13 November 2001, a US missile hit al-Jazeera's office in Kabul, Afghanistan, during the US invasion of that country.[38] On 8 April 2003, a US missile hit an electricity generator at al-Jazeera's office in Baghdad. The fire that erupted killed a reporter, Tareq Ayyoub, and wounded another staff member.[39]

Shamefully, as soon became apparent from the leak of the so-called 'al-Jazeera memo', the orders to bomb these offices appear to have come from the top of the American administration, from the very people who use the rhetoric of the *freedom of the press*. The al-Jazeera bombing memo is an unpublished memorandum emanating from within the British government purporting to be the minutes of a discussion between President Bush and Prime Minister Tony Blair, which took place on 16 April 2004 at the height of the US attack on Falluja, Iraq. The *Daily Mirror* published a story on its front page on 22 November 2005 claiming that the memo quotes Bush speculating about a US bombing raid on al-Jazeera's world headquarters in Doha as well as other locations. The story claimed that, in that instance, Blair persuaded Bush to take no action.[40] However, the BBC aired a story in 2001 on how the US Secretary of State Colin Powell told the Emir of Qatar, Sheikh Hamad Khalifa al-Thani, 'to rein in the influential and editorially independent Arab al-Jazeera television station, which gives airtime to anti-American opinions'.[41] This was similarly recommended by Frank J. Gaffney Jr, an individual who had held senior positions in the Reagan Defence Department and was the president of the Centre for Security Policy. In his article, 'Take Out Al Jazeera', he argued that 'it is imperative that enemy media be taken down if they insist on using their access to the airwaves as instruments of the war against us and our allies'.[42]

It comes as no surprise then that the United States, during the Bush presidency, has been falling down the rankings of the Worldwide Press Freedom Index, which is compiled by *Reporters Without Borders*. From a global position of 17th in 2002, the first year in which the index was compiled, the United States had fallen to 44th in 2005 and 53rd in 2006. Relations between the media and the Bush administration sharply deteriorated after the president used the pretext of 'national security' to regard as suspicious any journalist who questioned his 'War on Terrorism'.[43]

The media are left needing to ask themselves a series of difficult questions regarding their role in Bush's 'War on Terror'. Why did they fail to investigate the veracity claims of the wars that followed the 9/11 tragedy? Why did they fail to contribute to efforts to mediate peace given their vast potential to shape public opinion? And finally, what can be done in this age of 'broadcast democracy' to make media take centre stage in conflict resolution?

I conclude this chapter with the words of Walter Lippmann, ironically the man who first coined the term 'manufacture of consent', but whose essays on journalism and democracy, a little less than a century later, still have a lot of relevance to the practice of the profession.

> For the troubles of the press, like the troubles of representative government, be it territorial or functional, like the troubles of the industry, be it capitalist, cooperative or communist, go back to a common source: to the failure of self-governing people to transcend their casual experience and their prejudice, by inventing, creating, and organizing a machinery of knowledge. It is because they are compelled to act without a reliable picture of the world, that governments, schools, newspapers and churches make small headway against the more obvious failings of democracy, against violent prejudice, apathy, preference for the curious trivial as against the dull important, and the hunger for the sideshows and the three legged calves.[44]

Notes

1 Susan Carruthers, *The Media at War*, New York: Palgrave Macmillian, 2000, p. 16.
2 Walter Lippmann, 'Newspapers', *Public Opinion*, New York: Free Press, 1965, originally published 1922.
3 Jürgen Habermas, 'The Public Sphere', in Armand Mattelart and Seth Siegelaub (eds), *Communication and Class Struggle*, vol. 1, New York: International General, 1964, pp. 198–200.
4 Jürgen Habermas, 'Civil Society and the Political Public Sphere', *Between Facts and Norms: Contributions to a Discourse Theory of Law and Democracy*, Cambridge: MIT Press, 1996, pp. 359–87.
5 John M. Phelan, 'Selling Consent: The Public Sphere as a Televisual Market-place', in Peter Dahlgren and Colin Sparks (eds), *Communication and Citizenship: Journalism and the Public Sphere*, London: Routledge, 1991, p. 76.

6 Brett Silverstein, 'Toward a Science of Propaganda', *Political Psychology* 8 (1), 1987, pp. 49–59.
7 Leonard W. Doob, 'Goebbels' Principles of Propaganda', *The Public Opinion Quarterly* 14 (3), 1950, pp. 419–42.
8 John Perry, 'War Propaganda for Democracy', *The Public Opinion Quarterly* 6 (3), 1942, p. 438.
9 Charles A. H. Thomson, 'Overseas Information Service of the United States Government', Washington: Brookings Institution, 1948, pp. 53–5.
10 Bernard C. Cohen, *The Press and Foreign Policy*, Princeton, NJ: Princeton University Press, 1963, p. 13.
11 Denis McQuail, 'The Influence and Effects of Mass Communication', in J. Curran, M. Gurevitch and J. Woolacott (eds), *Mass Communication and Society*, London: Sage Publications, 1979, pp. 70–93.
12 Maxwell E. McCombs and Donald L. Shaw, 'The Agenda-Setting Functions of the Press', *Public Opinion Quarterly* 36, 1972, pp. 176–87.
13 Raymond Williams, *Marxism and Literature*, Oxford: Oxford University Press, 1977, p. 112.
14 Peter Dahlgren, 'The Third World on TV News: Western Ways of Seeing the Other', in W. C. Adams (ed.), *Television Coverage of International Affairs*, Norwood: Ablex, 1982, pp. 45–66.
15 Edward S. Herman and Noam Chomsky, *Manufacturing Consent: The Political Economy of the Mass Media*, New York: Pantheon, 1988, p. 2.
16 Herbert I. Schiller, *Information and the Crisis Economy*, New York: Oxford University Press, 1986, pp. 16–19.
17 Antony Giddens, 'The Nation-State and Violence', *Contemporary Critique of Historical Materialism*, vol. 2, Cambridge, UK: Polity Press, 1985, pp. 222–54.
18 David S. Alberts, John J. Garstka and Federick P. Stein, *Network Centric Warfare: Developing and Leveraging Information Superiority*, Washington, DC: CCRP Publication Series, 2005, pp. 2–10.
19 Ibid., p. 60.
20 Kenneth Payne, 'The Media as an Instrument of War', *Parameters* (Spring 2005), pp. 81, 93.
21 Antony Giddens, 'The Nation-State and Violence', *Contemporary Critique of Historical Materialism*, vol. 2, Cambridge, Polity Press, 1985, pp. 181–92.
22 Armand Mattelart, 'Notes on the Ideology of the Military State', in Armand Mattelart and Seth Siegelaub (eds), *Communication and Class Struggle*, vol. 1, New York: International General, 1978, pp. 403–7.
23 Armand Mattelart, 1978, p. 412.
24 Garth S. Jowett and Victoria O' Donnell, *Propaganda and Persuasion*, London: Sage, 1992, p. 4.
25 Mark Leonard, 'Diplomacy by Other Means', *Foreign Policy* 132, 2002, pp. 48–56.
26 Samuel Kernell, *Going Public: New Strategies of Presidential Leadership*, 3rd edn, Washington, DC, Congressional Quarterly, 1997.
27 Todd Gitlin, *The Whole World is Watching*, Berkeley: University of California Press, 1980, p. 7.
28 All three State of the Union addresses have been procured from the White House website.

29 CNN report, 'Some 9/11 families want Bush ads yanked', aired 6 March 2004, New York; http://www.whitehouse.gov/news/releases/2001/09/20010929.html.
30 Phil Rosenthal, 'Awe Arrives, But Not with Human Angle', *Chicago Sun-Times*, 22 March 2003.
31 Jean Baudrillard, *Ecstasy of Communication*, Paris: Semiotexte, 1988, p. 131.
32 Pierre Bourdieu, *On Television*, New York: The New Press, 1996, pp. 6–9.
33 Thomas E. Patterson, 'Political Roles of a Journalist', in Doris Graber, Denis McQuail and Pippa Norris (eds), *Politics of News: News of Politics*, Washington, DC: CQ Press, 1998, pp. 17–32.
34 Jorgen Westerstahl, 'Objective News Reporting', *Communication Research* 10 (3), 1983, pp. 403–24.
35 Lance W. Bennett, 'Toward a Theory of Press State Relations in the United States', *Journal of Communication* 40 (2), 1990, pp. 103–25.
36 Yoram Peri, 'Intractable Conflict and the Media', *Israel Studies* 12 (1), pp. 79–102.
37 James R. Compton, 'Shocked and Awed: The Convergence of Military and Media Discourse', Porto Alegre, Brazil: International Association for Media and Communication Research (IAMCR), 25–30 July 2004.
38 BBC report, 'Al-Jazeera Kabul offices hit in US raid', 13 November 2001.
39 BBC report, 'Al-Jazeera hit by missile', aired on 8 April 2003. For the link see http://news.bbc.co.uk/2/hi/middle_east/2927527.stm.
40 Kevin Maguire and Andy Lines, 'Bush plot to bomb his Arab ally', *Daily Mirror* (online), published on the cover page on 22 November 2005.
41 BBC report, 'US urges curb on Arab TV channel', BBC, 4 October 2001. See link: http://news.bbc.co.uk/2/hi/americas/1578619.stm.
42 Frank Gaffney, Jr, 'Take Out Al Jazeera', Centre for Security Policy website, 29 September 2003; http://www.foxnews.com/story/0,2933,98621,00.htm.
43 *Reporters Without Borders* compiled the Index by asking the 14 freedom-of-expression organizations that are its partners worldwide, its network of 130 correspondents, as well as journalists, researchers, jurists and human rights activists, to answer 50 questions about press freedom in their countries. The Index covers 168 nations.
44 Walter Lippmann, 'Newspapers', in *Public Opinion*, New York: Free Press, 1965, originally published 1922.

5

Image Culture, Media and Power

Khalid Hajji

Unlike 'old' cultures that resorted to poetry and oral tradition to come to terms with the world, our modern cultures use images to cope with reality in the age of globalization. Indeed, we often hear it said that we live in the age of an 'image culture'. If by 'image culture' we mean a space where the human eye is exposed to an endless flow of images, then the label is indeed befitting. However, doubt persists as to whether these images provide the mind with the intellectual force or moral moorings that would facilitate its coping with the state of 'discontent in civilization' of which we are victims. Images, no matter how expressive they might be, are weak carriers of meaning. Therefore, it is imperative to ask about the link between the state of meaninglessness that besets the context of our contemporary societies and the triumph of the visual over other modes of perception.

The increasing number of photographic stock agencies is one clear indication of the preponderant role played by images in our contemporary global culture. A photograph circulating the world gives wide-reaching visibility to an exhibited model. The impact of these visible exhibited models is not limited to the awakening of the impulse for consumption through different cultural contexts. Beyond this superficial level, the visible images contribute enormously to the flattening of the mindscape, paving the way for cultural hegemony, the despotism of political models and the triumph of one global market. However, if the link between 'image culture' and different forms of hegemony might seem self-evident, the roots of this culture remain concealed behind a cloak of images.

In his book *Bilder auf Weltreise*,[1] Wolfgang Ullrich provides us with very convincing examples of the correlation between the travelling images and the coercive forces of globalization. It was in the sixteenth-century Netherlands, in the first strongholds of capitalism, that the idea of commercializing images beyond the limits of one's own space and culture first saw the day. Unlike their Greek ancestors, who focused on the exaltation of healthy human bodies as a sign of the defiance of time, the modern European capitalists established another aim for their arts, namely that of transcending the limits of geography. A good work of art is one that can be sold everywhere, independent of the constraints of local tastes, space and geography. It is perhaps significant then that one of the first Dutch graphic publishers in the sixteenth century bears the name *Zu den vier Winden*, or 'to the four winds'.[2] One of the major concerns of Dutch artists of the period such as Rubens was the artistic conquest of the globe. Maps of the world and terrestrial globes conspicuously occupied the centre stage of many of their paintings, testifying to the artists' (and correspondingly the culture of their capitalist sponsors') growing interest in conquering the whole.

The examples cited in the work of Wolfgang Ullrich constitute noteworthy milestones in the history of the alliance that binds capitalism with 'image culture' in the age of globalization. However, the scope of Ullrich's critique of globalization does not allow for a deeper analysis of the roots of this alliance. A wider vista would reveal how the flourishing commerce of designs and images, besides epitomizing the triumph of the values of the market in the age of globalization, represents an unmistakable declaration of the demise of a culture that might be named *Dasein Culture*. By *Dasein Culture* we mean a culture where the senses of perception are equitably intensified and thus prevented from yielding to drowsiness.

Friedrich Nietzsche was alert enough to see that the progress promised by the European Renaissance and modernity would lead to crippled geniuses unable to live a fully sensuous life. In *Thus Spoke Zarathustra*[3] he writes the following:

> It is, however, the smallest thing unto me since I have been amongst men, to see one person lacking an eye, another an ear, and a third a leg, and that others have lost the tongue, or the nose, or the head. I see and have seen worse things, and divers things so hideous, that I should neither like to speak of all matters, nor even keep silent about some of them: namely, men who lack everything, except that they have too much of one thing – men who are nothing more than a big eye, or a big mouth, or a big belly, or something else big – reversed cripples, I call such men.

IMAGE CULTURE, MEDIA AND POWER

It is not an overstatement to say that the globalized design and image culture of our time is the epitome of the world described by Nietzsche, a world of reversed cripples, 'who lack everything, except that they have too much of one thing'. The design culture, which brought the demise of the *Dasein Culture*, has converted us into men and women who are nothing but big eyes.

Nietzsche articulated brilliantly the idea of a humanity disconnected from the real world and ensconced in an ersatz uni-dimensional reality. Indeed, the European Renaissance and the different forms of European enlightenments ushered in a new reality that can be grasped, in the first instance, through the sense of sight. Leonardo da Vinci, the visual mind of the Renaissance, is a perfect example of the afore-mentioned drive to antagonize the relationship between the senses. For this emblematic European figure of the Enlightenment, of the Renaissance and the modern world, the sense of sight should prevail when it comes to grasping the genuine aspects of reality. Images are much more telling than words, according to him. To writers, he gives the following piece of advice: 'O writer! What words can you find to describe the whole arrangement of the heart as perfectly as is done in this drawing? My advice is not to trouble yourself with words unless you are speaking to the blind.'[4] Da Vinci's advice announces the new reality that goes 'without saying', but not 'without seeing'. The lines quoted above suggest that the Enlightenment is associated with the visual mind, whereas words are remnants of a bygone era of blindness. The latter can no longer convey the meaning of the dawning reality.

The heirs to da Vinci's legacy of the visual thinking and reception of the world invented the camera, a tool that would extend the sense of vision beyond all expectations. The camera is indeed one of the most crucial breakthroughs in the history of sense perception; it is a device with an inestimable outreach for modern culture. It is no exaggeration to divide the history of human inventions into 'before' and 'after' the camera.

Before the camera, all attempts at mimicking reality, however talented the genius behind them, were dyed by the hues of subjectivity, disfigured and distorted by the brush of the painter or by the chisel of the sculptor. The hand of the craftsman used, so to say, to tamper with reality. This, by necessity, created a gap and a distance between its input and its output. For the eyes of the beholder, the object of painting or sculpture might be less beautiful than its imitation, but it can never be less close to reality. The real object enjoys more credibility. With the lens of the camera, on the other hand, all is different. A photographic shot increases the sense of perfect depiction and rendering, for the art of photography is not a manual one. It is an art of revelation. The camera reveals the truth of the object without tampering with it, hence its credibility in the eyes of the receiver.

With the art of photography, a major step was taken towards the portrayal of the 'other' and the subduing of his reality to the prisms of the visual perception. Now the other strikes us as a visual reality beyond suspicion. Before the camera era, for example, Mary Wortley Montagu lamented the lot of Western travellers visiting Constantinople, as follows: 'We travellers are in very hard circumstances: If we say nothing but what has been said before us, we are dull and we have observed nothing. If we tell any thing new, we are laughed at as fabulous and romantic . . .'[5] Following the invention of the camera, however, the beholder could see and believe. The art of photography freed Western travellers of the dilemma they experienced between the 'boring dullness' of repeating what was known and risking disbelief in the novelty and originality of their accounts. One photograph in the hand is worth thousands of pages of words in books. Never before had the accounts about other spaces been so close to objective experience as with this new art. It is true that the Orient has been related and narrated by talented masters of the quill pen, or painted by highly gifted painters. Nevertheless, all attempts at convincingly depicting the space of the other remained tinged with a streak of subjectivity, compared with the art of photography, which strongly enhances the sense of neutral objective perception of the outside world.

With every new technical development, the art of photography gained in expressivity, eloquence, sharpness and the replication in images of life, thereby championing multi-dimensional visual over linear verbal thinking. However, it was not until the discovery of the motion picture camera that the circle of dominance was completed. The recording of moving images allows not only the freezing of a moving object into an unchangeable identity, but also the subduing of historical processes, stories and narratives. Armed with this new device, the traveller, the Orientalist, the tourist or the spy is capable of visual narration of the other's stories. The other is caught in movement, in progress. The close-up technique allows the furtive inquisitive eye to rummage in the space of the other, while the replay technique enables it to revisit its time and probe into its folds and wrinkles. In brief, every new device constitutes an extension of the eye's capabilities as well as an increase in reliability and credibility in reproducing reality. Thus, after the war of images, came a war of visual narratives.

All the technological forays that expanded the visual field notwithstanding, it may be safely affirmed that the question of meaning is still not resolved. The vastness of covered realities, explored events and reported stories and profiles does not make any significant difference concerning the understanding of the world and our place in it. Even though at first glance filming and photographing strikes the receiver as being an impartial art of revelation, the truth is that the eye of the film-maker and the photographer meddles in plenty of ways with the so-called revealed reality. Every image or sequence of images is nothing but the outcome of an elaborate effort of selection; it delimits by necessity the scope of perception and obeys the dialectics of outside and inside, exclusion and inclusion. As such, the art of the visual revelation is liable to fall prey to the hegemonic drive whenever it is predicated upon the old foolish assumption that the realm of the inside can enclose the diversity of the outside. In fact, of all the models of sense perception, nothing can be more tyrannical than an image culture driven only by the impulse of human reason to unity and comprehension.

A short dialogue between Lawrence of Arabia and some Bedouin Arabs exemplifies the idea that, whatever our technical ingenuity and sophisticated know-how, we remain far from reaching the bedrock of some cosmic reality. Lawrence keeps a record of this conversation as follows:

> Nasir rolled over on his back, with my glasses, and began to study the stars, counting aloud first one group and then another; crying out with surprise at discovering little lights not noticed by his unaided eye. Auda set us on to talk of telescopes – of the great ones – and of how man in three hundred years had so far advanced from his first essay that now he built glasses as long as a tent, through which he counted thousands of unknown stars. 'And the stars – what are they?' We slipped into talk of suns beyond suns, sizes and distance beyond wit. 'What will now happen with this knowledge?' asked Mohammed.
>
> We shall set to, and many learned and some clever men together will make glasses as more powerful than ours, as ours than Galileo's; and yet more hundreds of astronomers will distinguish and reckon yet

more thousands of now unseen stars, mapping them, and giving each one its name. When we see them all, there will be no night in heaven.

'Why are the Westerners always wanting all?' provokingly said Auda. 'Behind our few stars we can see God, who is not behind your millions.' 'We want the world's end, Auda.' 'But that is God's', complained Zaal, half angry. Mohammed would not have his subject turned. 'Are there men on these greater worlds?' he asked. 'God knows.' 'And has each the Prophet and heaven and hell?' Auda broke in on him. 'Lads, we know our districts, our camels, our women. The excess and the glory are to God. If the end of wisdom is to add star to star our foolishness is pleasing.'[6]

The lesson drawn from this conversation is that continuous forays in the realm of the unseen and the extension of the visual tools of perception are not enough to endow the mapped reality with meaning. Wisdom, indeed, does not consist in adding star to star. It is one thing to say that the modern mass media have the most sophisticated equipment to dissect both space and time. Much as the close-up techniques allow the exploration of the wrinkles of spatial reality, the replay techniques snatch the fleeting moment from the grip of time and subdue it to visual scrutiny. Yet it is quite another thing to extract sense and value from what is seen. Self-referential images, or images that feed on other images, distract the mind more than they provide it with meaning. The images of video clips, for example, are the epitome of this type of meaninglessness and insignificance. Once detached from meaning, they, in their turn, contribute to disconnect the mind from reality.

Along with the general scepticism, engendered by the horrific European wars of the twentieth century, grows uncertainty and doubt concerning the capacity of the sense of sight 'to make sense of the world'. Indeed, a new change in the history of sense perception is in the offing in the works of some highly energetic intellectual figures of the twentieth century. Antoine de Saint-Exupéry, an intellectual trying to fathom what has gone wrong in Western civilization, writes the following in his classical work *Le Petit Prince*:[7]

> 'Goodbye', said the fox. 'And now here is my secret, a very simple secret: It is only with the heart that one can see rightly; what is essential is invisible to the eye.'
>
> 'What is essential is invisible to the eye', the little prince repeated, so that he would be sure to remember.

This intellectual attitude ushers in a new era, opening a new horizon. The field of visual perception opened by da Vinci is deemed to be of little avail in pointing at the essence of things. The intellectual endeavour to enclose truth and to essentialize identities, be it through the senses or through human reason, is no longer appealing. The visual order imposed upon the world has shuttered into insignificance. Now the question of the alternative is more urgent than ever before. The new quest is titled 'postmodern', and the human mind faces the old 'primitive' questions anew. Even if we get to the heart of the matter, see it, explore it, touch it, meaning will always be drifting past our understanding; for the world, as we are told, is perpetually in becoming. A picture, an image, be it physical or mental, cannot convey anything essential about existence. As Kenneth White writes:

> Even if we had only those few scattered rocks on the shore,
> (The wind tonight blowing hard with rain over the sea)
> How much
> There would be to be learned
> For it is possible
> To live with the rocks
> In unity of mind
> And perhaps the one who knows
> Even one rock thoroughly
> In all its idiosyncrasies
> And relatedness to sea and sky
> Is better fit to speak
> To another human being
> Than someone who lives and rots perpetually
> In a crowded city
> That teaches him nothing essential.[8]

Ever since the middle of nineteenth century, some intellectual figures of Western culture have voiced their concern that what they have been seeking remains still not found. I think here, for example, of Walt Whitman and his poem where he faces the West from California's shores:

> Facing west from California's shores,
> Inquiring, tireless, seeking what is yet unfound,
> I, a child, very old, over waves, towards the house of maternity,
> the land of migrations, look afar,
> Look off the shores of my Western sea, the circle almost circled;

> For starting westward from Hindustan, from the vales of Kashmere,
> From Asia, from the north, from the God, the sage, and the hero,
> From the south, from the flowery peninsulas and the spice islands,
> Long having wander'd since, round the earth having wander'd,
> Now I face home again, very pleas'd and joyous,
> (But where is what I started for so long ago? And why is it
> yet unfound?).⁹

Unfortunately, the concerns and worries articulated by Whitman and intellectual figures of his ilk have not given way to a recognizable mainstream quest for meaning. While the issue of meaning remains the matter of the few who dive below, the mainstream global culture is an endless show where models of success, beauty, youth and wealth are exposed. The image culture is now a design culture meant to swindle the eye of the beholder into purchasing things already had. The object is pulled out of shape and commoditized, not for its functions but for the new colours and forms that add to its 'aesthetic value'. So the triumph of the image culture epitomizes the triumph of the market and its subservient political forces. The exhibited images in the media both delimit the world of politics and political action by 'citifying' the awareness and the identity of the human being, and promote models of beauty and aesthetic values to market commodified items and further consumerism. The prevalence of the sense of sight has smoothed the progress of capitalism and globalization. It has been fatally detrimental to the critical mind. Thus it suffices it to put on display one image in a United Nations plenary session, and you can justify a terrible and frightening war, as happened before the invasion of Iraq.

We understand from what has been said that the dominant Western image culture is anchored in a philosophical context, the ideas of which face a serious challenge in the postmodern era. To reassemble the fragments of the story of this culture, it is useful to start with a reference to Raphael's painting *The School of Athens*. At the centre of this painting are both Plato and Aristotle. The former points to the sky with his extended index finger, while the latter invites us to touch the earth with the palm of his hand facing down. No doubt, the portrayal of the School of Athens hints at one fundamental debate in the history of Western thought, namely the debate between idealists and realists. While the idealists, followers of Plato, assume that the truth is in the sky, beyond the reach of our senses, the realists, the followers of

Aristotle, would content themselves with the earth and with the truth that emanates from it. The drawing of the two Greek masters magnifies the significance of the School of Athens' legacy, and emphasizes the fact that the Renaissance mind is an heir to the traditional battle which, in depth, beyond the antithesis of idealism and realism, opposes the two major senses, the sense of hearing and the sense of sight. While Platonic idealism assigns merit to words capable of carrying the meaning of the absent reality through the sense of audition, Aristotelian realism is an attempt at submitting language to the diktat of the visual reality.

In other words, the so-called image culture is the outcome of a long debate between idealism and realism. This debate has antagonized the relationship between the senses and ended up championing the belief in the capability of the sense of sight to embrace the truth of the living. Indeed, the role of other senses receded to the advantage of the inquisitive eye, the result being an endless flow of colours, shapes, images and designs that try to outline reality. However, the tremendous achievements of image culture have not contributed to the carrying of any fundamental meaning. On the contrary, the extolled image culture has contributed to the destruction of meaning, to the trivialization of culture, to the numbing of the senses, and to the shrinking of critical thinking.

Media in the age of image culture

Driven by the instinct to vie for audiences in the swiftly changing world of globalization, the mass media nonetheless still exudes confidence in the power of images to portray or express 'the Truth'. Locked in a bitter struggle for survival, the major media institutions around the world have, in fact, no time to reconsider their relation to the image culture, to rethink the impact of images on cosmically disoriented masses, or to scrutinize the conceptual basis upon which their recourse to images is predicated. In a sense, the mass media – especially news television – are the perfect embodiment of a hegemonic impulse that confines truth to what is seen. Even when they do not declare it, they nurture the illusion of a possible 'inclusiveness'. All the scattered elements of truth are pulled together into one visual whole.

A cursory glance at contemporary mass media betrays a stark endeavour to endow images with argumentative power. Images are indeed the backbone of media rhetoric, the backdrop against which media narratives develop and advance. They can be anything but a neutral, objective rendering of reality. Much as truth is reduced in the modern visual media to images, awareness is coerced into a world political order and a restricted conceptual framework of reference. Far from revealing the truth of anything, the circulating images reflect the reality of the contending powers in the context of globalization. They can be divided into two categories: either part of a 'coercive rhetoric' or part of a 'resistance rhetoric'. The new technical developments and breakthroughs in the field of filming and photographing do not free the media of today from this rhetorical stalemate. Whether they are images relating to the conflict that sets Palestinians against Israelis, Chinese against Tibetans, the United States against the countries of the so-called Axis of Evil, or the West against the Rest of the world, they mirror existing balances of power and their games of coercion and resistance.

Basically, the future of the relationship between media and image culture is shaped by the contending political and economic powers around the globe. Neither the neutrality of images nor the power of the media are sustainable myths. Both image and media are tools subjugated to the whims and wills of powerful political and economical institutions. Images are far from reflecting reality; rather they construct it by sheer acts of inclusion and exclusion. This said, it becomes incumbent upon the media to face the moral duty of building a possible different world, instead of contenting themselves with the old, fallacious assertion that the imitation of reality is possible.

Rethinking the relationship between media and image culture on the one hand, and media and power on the other, is a fundamental necessity. If we admit that the effusion of images in our cultural context does not carry to the viewer any novel sense of being outside the coercive political and economical orders, it is imperative to envisage other possible alternatives. One original alternative would be to dyke up the flow of images that besiege the human awareness. Undoubtedly, an economical use of visual media will further mental lucidity, psychological placidity and critical thinking; for the incessant exposure to shapes, colours, models, designs and scenes plays a major role in the disconnection of the human mind from its contextual reality and in the numbing of the senses. More than any time before in the history of visual culture, the world seems to suffer from being almost fully saturated with images. Life has turned out to depend utterly on visibility. The more visible you are, the more living you feel.

The essential role of the media is by no means to provide the contending political and economic powers with visibility. On the contrary, what they ought to do is to mediate between the different existing forces in the world: between the 'Self' and the 'Other', the 'Self' and the 'World' or 'Nature', and the 'Self' and the 'Unknown'. Of course, images can play one important role in this mediation, but not an exclusive one. To remind the human mind of the lost existential dimensions, or to hint at the existence of 'unknown modes of being', would require other vehicles of meaning. It is necessary in this respect to think about rehabilitating verbal culture, a verbal culture with a strong sense of the word. At the height of postmodern disorientation, humanity is in need of words to rediscover the world.

NOTES

1. Wolfgang Ullrich, *Bilder auf Weltreise: Eine Globalisierungskritik*, Berlin: Wagenbach, 2006.
2. Ibid., p. 12.
3. Friedrich Nietzsche, *Thus Spoke Zarathustra*, London: Penguin Classics, 1969, p. 159.
4. Lisa Jardine, 'Breaking the Da Vinci code', *The Guardian*, 27 November 2004.
5. Mary Wortley Montagu, *Letters from the Right Honourable Lady Mary Wortley Montagu 1709 to 1762*, London: J. M. Dent., 1906 (first published 1763).
6. T. E. Lawrence, *Seven Pillars of Wisdom*, Ware, Hertfordshire: Wordsworth Editions, 1997, p. 273.
7. Antoine de Saint-Exupéry, *The Little Prince*, trans. Katherine Woods, New York: Reynal and Hitchcock, 1943, chapter 21.
8. Kenneth White, *A Walk Along the Shore*, éd. bilingue, trans. Patrick Guyon and Marie-Claude White, Paris: Mercure de France, 1979, pp. 118–19.
9. Walt Whitman, 'Facing West from California's Shores', *The Complete Poems*, Harmondsworth: Penguin, 1986, p. 145.

6

Religious Diaspora and Information Communications Technology: The Impact of Globalization on Communal Relations in Egypt

Fiona McCallum

Introduction

The development of 'new media' as an aspect of the wider globalization process has had a wide-ranging impact on the Middle East region. In particular, information and communication technologies (ICTs) provide marginalized groups with an opportunity to publicize their political agenda. Initially, there was perhaps an over-optimistic belief that this new media would be the vanguard of a revolution bringing democratic change to one of the last bastions of authoritarianism in the post-Cold War world. The expansion of the public sphere coupled with a newly thriving civil society would lead to a 'bottom-up' approach whereby the public would be able to shape political developments in the region. However, as Norton aptly notes, it would be 'wishful thinking to presume that new media are in themselves an antidote to authoritarianism'.[1] Instead, regimes have been able to maintain a significant amount of control and ensured that the new media has been incorporated into existing power structures.[2] However, it cannot be denied that information and communication technology has had an impact on the political environment. Diaspora groups have often been the most active as they have access to this technology and frequently have the political freedom to utilize its potential both in advocating their cause and also in communicating with members in the homeland and throughout the diaspora.

This chapter seeks to address the implications of the spread of this new media on Middle Eastern politics by examining the experience of the Coptic community. The Copts are an indigenous group located in

Egypt whose significant distinguishing feature from the Muslim majority is their Christian faith. In general, Egypt has experienced harmonious communal relations marred by occasional violent incidents. However, the use of information technology by émigré groups in their campaigns to protect Coptic rights has been interpreted as a challenge to the status quo and has the potential to lead to the deterioration of Christian–Muslim relations in Egypt. In a less provocative but equally influential manner, this new media has also served to accentuate Coptic identity, which can adversely affect the 'national unity' rhetoric enlisted by the government when commenting on communal harmony. Furthermore, the Coptic Orthodox Church – the main communal institution and regarded as the protector of Coptic faith and identity – has utilized the same aspects of globalization to promote its leadership role over the entire community, including the diaspora. Thus, the Coptic case offers a new perspective on the role of information and communications technology in the Middle East – one in which elements within distinct communal groups, including those in the diaspora, can use the fruits of the globalization process to become independent actors and consequently attain the ability to affect the political landscape of the homeland.

Globalization and the diaspora
Globalization is widely recognized as having challenged conventional views regarding state sovereignty and territorial boundaries. Defined by Scholte as 'processes whereby many social relations became relatively detached from territorial geography, so that human lives are increasingly played out in the world as a single place',[3] this emphasis on deterritorialization has allocated a greater role to transnational actors in the international political arena. According to Mandaville, 'globalization has also given birth to transnational actors on a global scale which is historically unprecedented: ethnic minorities, diaspora groups and migrant workers are all examples of this phenomenon'.[4] Such actors have benefited from developments in transport and information technology. Travel has now become possible for all rather than restricted to the wealthy few, and the information revolution has led to wide accessibility to television and the Internet. Consequently, the 'global village' not only allows people in one region to witness events in another but also enables them to maintain constant contact through electronic mail and Internet chat sites.

Furthermore, globalization has accentuated the importance of culture. Instead of solely producing a Western-dominated homogeneous culture as was initially predicted, local cultures have also been reinvigorated. Robertson describes this twofold process as the 'interpenetration of the universalization of particularism and the particularization of universalism'.[5] Together, these developments have combined to create an environment where diaspora communities can flourish and retain their links to the homeland to the extent that they constitute an active though not physical presence in the political arena.

Diaspora groups have increasingly become international actors in the globalization era. In the past, the distance and separation meant that immigrants became dislocated from their home country. Although they normally retained aspects of their heritage, integration into their new political culture often took precedence over participation in homeland politics. However, globalization has encouraged the holding of multiple identities, meaning that immigrants no longer have to choose one loyalty at the expense of the other. Furthermore, this also allows other identities, including religious affiliation, to be regarded as compatible with national identity. The literature on the political role of the diaspora normally focuses on ethnonationalist groups and limits religious diasporas to global faiths (e.g., Islam and Catholicism) or those which overlap with a distinctive ethnic identity (e.g., the Armenians).[6] A consensus has not been reached on determining the criteria that distinguishes a diaspora from an expatriate community. Van Hear argues that three requirements must be met: the population is dispersed from the homeland to other lands, there is a continual presence abroad and there is an exchange between the dispersed populations.[7] Other suggestions include the retention of a collective memory of the homeland and a desire to eventually return.[8] Clearly, using the above criteria, groups that are distinguished solely through their religious identity, such as the case study used in this paper, have the potential to act as a diaspora and hence can benefit from the tools of the globalization process in attaining their objective of participating as an independent actor in homeland politics.

The Coptic Orthodox community in Egypt and abroad

The Coptic community is synonymous with the state of Egypt. Indeed, the term Copt is derived from the Greek *aigyptos*, meaning Egypt.[9] The

Coptic community today consists of the descendants of the original Christian population in Egypt prior to the Arab Conquest in the seventh century, who resisted the attractions of converting to Islam – the official state religion.[10] The Copts are the largest Christian community in the Middle East, estimated to number between five and six million. As is the case with most minority groups in the region, population figures prove controversial. These statistics range from 5 per cent of the Egyptian population (academic research) and 10 per cent (Coptic Orthodox Church) to inflated claims of 15–20 per cent (expatriate groups).[11] Regardless of the exact amount, there is a clear and visible Coptic presence in Egypt. They are found in all social classes and all regions. While some still live in rural areas, many Copts, like their Muslim compatriots, have been affected by the urbanization trend in modern Egyptian society. The main (and often only) distinguishing feature is their religious affiliation. The vast majority of Copts belong to the Coptic Orthodox Church, although there is also a Coptic Catholic Church and several Protestant denominations. Thus, the former can be regarded as a national church in the sense that most Egyptian Christians are members and there are few adherents outside Egypt who are not of Egyptian heritage.[12] Furthermore, it is the only communal institution that includes the entire Coptic Orthodox community. Under the traditional 'millet' system of managing communal relations, the head of the church, the Patriarch of Alexandria and all Africa (currently Patriarch Shenouda III), is recognized by the Egyptian government as the spokesman and representative of the community.[13]

This situation partly reflects the transition from the vibrant party system in the 1920s, when Copts were influential in the Wafd Party, to the authoritarian political system in place since 1952, which has limited the ability of Copts to succeed through the electoral process. Indeed, it is common practice for the president to include several Copts as part of his ten appointees to parliament. While Coptic participation in politics may be limited, they are active in other fields, including medicine and business. The main Coptic concerns relate to perceptions of discrimination such as the laws (and practicalities) involving church buildings and conversions. These two issues are often the underlying cause of the third Coptic concern – violence perpetrated against Copts.[14] In general, the Coptic community ascribes to the idea of national unity proclaimed by the Egyptian government.

All Middle Eastern Christian communities have been affected by the curse of emigration – a trend that in some cases can threaten the future viability of the group in retaining a significant presence in the region. The Coptic case is slightly different, considering the actual size of the community and the relatively late commencement of emigration. This coincided with the nationalization policies instigated by President Nasser in the 1950s. These affected the wealthy Coptic landowning and business elite, resulting in members of these families turning their attention to countries outside of the Middle East in order to improve their prospects. They were soon followed by other members of the community, predominantly young educated professionals. While this same trend is present among Egyptian Muslims, the number of Copts in proportion to the size of their community means that this process has more impact on the community as a whole. This brain-drain is likely to continue as each new group of émigrés creates networks to aid newcomers, thus actually serving to encourage emigration. Again, there are no acknowledged statistics of the Coptic expatriate community. Estimates vary from 400,000 to one million. Favoured destinations include Canada, the United States, Latin American, Australia and Europe. This steady flow of emigration has created the conditions for the formation of a Coptic diaspora. Coptic communities can be regarded as part of the Egyptian diaspora while simultaneously forming their own diaspora. There is a distinct homeland as well as a collective identity. Communal organizations have been created partly to assist members integrating into the host society, and partly to establish frequent contact both with the homeland and between the expatriate communities in different countries.[15] Coptic migrant political activity has tended to focus on the homeland, mostly as there has been little resistance to their integration into host societies and they have been able to retain their cultural identity and heritage. From the beginning, expatriate groups have utilized the media in order to publicize their campaigns. In the tense Sadat years in the late 1970s, émigré lobbying contributed to the decision of the government to abandon the 1977 apostasy bill. During Sadat's visit to the United States in 1980, expatriates organized street demonstrations and ran newspaper adverts protesting against the situation of the Copts in Egypt. In reality, these actions only served to influence Sadat against the community, leading to his decision to banish Patriarch Shenouda to a desert monastery in 1981.[16] However, they gave an indication of the impact that émigré groups could have, even before the groundbreaking developments of the Internet and satellite television.

Numerous Coptic expatriate lobby groups have been formed by migrants in host societies. While these can be found wherever there is a Coptic presence, the most active are in North America and Australia. Their main objective is to protect Coptic rights. Aware of the importance of the human rights agenda in the international community, activists have campaigned within this framework. Their premise is that by demonstrating that human rights violations are occurring in Egypt against Copts, Western governments will have no choice but to pressurize the Egyptian regime to address this situation. In particular, they argue that US aid to Egypt should be conditional on respecting the human rights of Christians in Egypt. For example, Coptic activists were strong supporters of the US Congress International Religious Freedom Act, which was passed in 1998. This legislation was an indication of international commitment to religious freedom and created the position of Ambassador at Large for International Religious Freedom as well as producing an annual report on International Religious Freedom.[17] Representatives of Coptic organizations met with congressional committees and placed adverts in the national media detailing the 'oppression of Copts in Egypt' during the congressional hearings.

The formation of Coptic groups often follows a recognized pattern. One ardent individual who has attained financial success in his area of expertise uses his wealth to set up an organization to campaign for Coptic rights. These different activists tend not to coordinate regular activities. In some cases, the organization is considered solely as a 'shell' to advance the interests and public recognition of the founder. Others have developed into well-structured organizations with staff, coordinated and professional campaigns and media facilities. Notable groups include the US Copts Association, the Middle East Christians Association, the American Coptic Association and Copts United.[18] Although the primary approach has been to challenge the Egyptian government through pressure from the West, especially the US, these groups have not been particularly successful in making an impact on US administrations. US aid to Egypt has on the whole remained unchanged. Instead, some organizations have developed ties with individual politicians who support their campaigns within the context of combating 'religious persecution'. Thus, they are in a position to take advantage of any wider governmental interest in these issues. In contrast, Coptic émigré groups have had a more visible, though not necessarily positive, impact on their homeland. Annual conferences held to discuss the 'Coptic situation' attract attention in the Egyptian media and are often erroneously described as being sponsored by the US government. These events routinely culminate in resolutions calling for more US pressure against Egypt, including the restriction of aid. Invited speakers are often figures identified in the Arab world as being pro-Israeli and anti-Muslim. It is debatable how representative these lobby groups are of the entire Coptic expatriate community. In fact, it is generally recognized that activists are a small proportion of the overall diaspora. However, it is the above-mentioned vocal groups that receive significant attention in Egypt. One of the main reasons why they have triggered such a response is due to their extensive use of the Internet as a means both to reduce the distance between Egypt and their countries of residence and also to disseminate their views on events occurring in Egypt.

The impact of diaspora use of the Internet
The émigré groups that attract media coverage in Egypt are similar in the sense that their activities are primarily web-based. Their virtual presence fulfils various functions. First, each website provides a history of the Coptic Church and people, and, following tradition, tends to emphasize the martyrdom themes prevalent in Coptic history. Second, by presenting both Arabic- and English-language pages, the organizations try to bridge the gap between the homeland and host countries. The Arabic site allows those in Egypt to access the information, while the English pages cater both for emigrants without sufficient Arabic skills and, more importantly, for members of the international community interested in finding out more information about the Copts. In some cases, the sites offer direct links to the official Coptic Orthodox Church, including the weekly sermons given by Patriarch Shenouda, thereby demonstrating the close link between the Church and the community. Third, many of the organizations provide discussion forums, which serve to allow members to share their opinions on events in Egypt. Finally, and perhaps the most relevant aspect for this study, the websites act as news information services, reporting on the latest developments affecting Copts in Egypt. Reports from professional news

agencies, as well as from Western organizations that focus on the persecution of Christians (such as Compass Direct), are posted on these sites. Through the technological benefits of the Internet, émigré groups are able to instantly publicize this information, sometimes accompanied by photographic evidence of the aftermath of a violent incident. It is this 'real-time' element that creates problems with the Egyptian authorities, media and public opinion. Reports are rarely verified by those in the diaspora. News articles posted directly by the organization tend to be characterized by inflammatory language, are prone to exaggeration and often fail to verify the details. Furthermore, each report is viewed through the perspective of the émigrés, i.e., within a persecution framework that sees every incident as proof of discrimination which is condoned and possibly practised by the Egyptian regime. Indeed, the mission statement of the US Copts Association says that discrimination and violence against the Copts 'are the products of intentional and/or neglectful practices of both the Egyptian government and various groups of misguided and misinformed Muslims'.[19]

The publicity surrounding each event follows the same pattern: the violence is blamed on 'Muslim fanatics', all incidents are viewed as part of a wider religious conflict, the Copts are presented as innocent victims and the government reaction is denounced as weak and inconsequential. Positive developments such as the easing of restrictive legislation relating to church building and repair permits and the recognition of Coptic Christmas as a national holiday in 2003 receive little positive comment and instead are regarded sceptically by the activists, who question the motives behind such moves. In order to illustrate how these predetermined assumptions colour reports on the Coptic situation in Egypt, two issues will be examined: conversion, and the violent incidents that occurred in the village of al-Kush.

There is a steady flow of reports about Coptic girls who convert to Islam. These are almost always reported on the émigré lobby groups' websites as forced conversions, i.e., kidnappings. A typical press release details the anguish of the girl's family and the hostility they encounter when they report the incident to the police, and indicates that state officials either collude with the 'kidnappers' or, at best, refuse to intervene on behalf of the Coptic family.[20] The reality is far more complex than this approach would suggest. While many claims of forced conversions arise, evidence is rarely provided to substantiate these accusations. Investigations by non-governmental organizations into several of these cases present a different story.[21] The Coptic girls in question are often young, sometimes trying to escape a strict household, and usually want to convert in order to marry a Muslim boyfriend. While this is not strictly required under sharia law, conversion ensures inheritance rights and increases the prospects of successful integration into her new family. This is particularly important, as her own family are likely to disown her if the conversion is seen as her own choice.

Conversion is clearly a public issue in Egypt. Changing from one faith to another is often regarded as proof of the superiority of that specific faith. Hence, it has been argued that this unwillingness to accept that Copts may choose to convert leads to rumours that the person in question must have been tricked and coerced into the situation. There is no denying that the environment in Egypt is conducive to conversion to Islam. It is the official state religion, the process is straightforward, and the convert may find their socio-economic conditions improve. It is estimated that around 10,000 Egyptian Christians convert to Islam each year, often due to social and economic factors.[22] Regarding Coptic girls, some reported cases are underage. By Egyptian law, a woman under 18 who wishes to marry requires parental consent. Furthermore, a convert is supposed to meet with a member of the clergy to ascertain that it is their desire to change religion. Frequently, these conditions are not fulfilled. However, while Muslim groups are certainly active in proselytizing among Egyptian Christians, there is a difference between offering spiritual and material inducements to convert and 'kidnapping'. Yet these events are regularly reported by émigré groups with no regard to the context of the individual case and, most importantly, are picked up by Western Christian movements, human rights organizations and even international media as authentic reports on the discrimination practised against Christians in Egypt.

The second category of reports that are frequently posted on émigré websites relates to violent incidents. Many of these are connected to Muslim suspicion of Christian attempts to build churches, often converting a house or church-owned building into a place of worship without official permission – permission that can be extremely difficult to obtain.[23] The most notable engagement of émigré lobby sites, however, concerned two incidents in the Christian-majority village of al-Kush in Upper Egypt. In 1998, two Christians were murdered, allegedly as part of a gambling vendetta. Police forces questioned some 500 Copts, which was interpreted by some as an indication of the authorities' desire to find a Coptic suspect in order to avert any communal unrest. Allegations of police brutality and torture were rife during this incident and reported by human rights organizations. In particular, the local Coptic Orthodox bishop, Wissa, was prominent in making these claims. The Coptic lobby groups chose to present this as persecution of Copts condoned by the Egyptian government, a theme that was reiterated by the international media.[24] This led to a furious reaction within Egypt over the fact that mass arrests and police brutality – an unwelcome but common occurrence, especially when dealing with lower social classes – had been transformed into evidence of persecution.

In this poisoned atmosphere, it was not surprising that a dispute between a Christian shopkeeper and Muslim customer escalated into violence that left 19 Christians and one Muslim dead, over 40 injured, and Christian homes and shops attacked in 2000.[25] The local government authorities were criticized for their slow response which allowed the violence to continue over three days and spread to a neighbouring village. In the aftermath of this incident, several trials were held but the vast majority of defendants were acquitted. Furthermore, continuing the tradition of trying to appear neutral, 38 Christians were charged, although the other group was widely regarded as instigating the conflict.

The failure of the Egyptian judicial system to obtain convictions was denounced by many groups and individuals, including Patriarch Shenouda and Muslim intellectuals. However, the US Copts Association interpreted these denouncements as proof of the government's culpability and discussed this matter under headlines such as 'The Egyptian Regime Encourages Persecution of Coptic Christians'.[26] Michael Meunier, the Association's president, also investigated the possibility of proceeding with the case through the International Criminal Court at The Hague.[27]

The quest to attain justice for the al-Kush victims remains a priority for the émigré groups. A recent movement, the Middle Eastern Christians Association, which was established in 2006, has instructed lawyers to commence compensation claims in the Egyptian civil courts on behalf of the villagers.[28] By focusing on the above type of incidents, diaspora organizations evoke an image of Egypt as a country where its Christian community is subject to frequent and violent attacks, vulnerable to orchestrated attempts to challenge its religious affiliation, and receiving minimal assistance from the state.

While conversions, church building and violence remain key concerns of the Coptic community both in Egypt and the diaspora, this exclusive focus ignores the many positive encounters that Copts experience in Egypt. As will be explored shortly, the constant negativity espoused by émigré activists provokes strong condemnation in Egypt and raises tension between the two communities.

Satellite television and the Coptic community

The other form of new media, satellite television, is also becoming a medium for Egyptian Christians – both in Egypt and the diaspora. Although in this case study it is less developed than the use of web technology, émigré activists are becoming aware of its potential. Such use of satellite television by non-state actors has not attracted substantial scholarly attention. Instead, research on this area has predominantly focused on the impact of the groundbreaking news channel al-Jazeera and subsequent competitors.[29] However, it has been acknowledged that satellite television can be used by regional and ethnic groups to accentuate their own identity. Sakr provides an interesting discussion on the short-lived MED TV in the mid-1990s, which was an attempt to create a 'virtual Kurdistan'. The objection of the Turkish authorities, who dubbed the channel 'PKK TV in disguise', led to the eventual suspension of its licence.[30]

This example illustrates the predicted response of Middle Eastern governments to the creation of private media stations associated with a specific group. Governments are already aware of the challenge to their authority posed by satellite television. According to Ghareeb, they provide competition for the official and predominantly state-owned channels, reach the illiterate sector of the population which is inaccessible to other forms of information technology, and thus make the elite more vulnerable.[31] Indeed, this type of media has been utilized by dissidents as a means to reach a potential audience at home. Sakr explains that channels privately owned by wealthy emigrants are 'clearly born out of the need for a political player in a specific Middle Eastern country to pursue his bid for power from a foreign base because of the constraints on political activity at home'.[32] This challenge is heightened further when considering distinct ethnic or religious communities. The airing of a channel exclusively designed to appeal to them is likely to heighten group identity, often at the expense of national identity. Furthermore, satellite television transcends territorial boundaries, linking the community at home with members of the diaspora. It is also a two-sided process. The medium can be used by the diaspora to inform the community of specific events and issues, but equally it can be directed towards the diaspora to reinvigorate its cultural identity and retain links with the homeland. In order to achieve this, the community requires wealthy benefactors who are willing to invest in this type of project.

Copts have not been immune to these changes occurring within the region. Although Egypt has been at the forefront of the 'satellite revolution' and has a state-owned satellite Nilesat, this does not include 'Christian' channels. Theoretically, religious channels are not allowed to be aired on Nilesat. Widely perceived as Islamic, the two channels, however, are categorized as 'general channels with religious inclinations' and are thus permitted to be shown.[33] Instead, Copts in Egypt have become attached to stations aimed at Middle Eastern Christians, including al-Hayat which is based in Cyprus.[34] This channel has proven controversial, as certain programmes are considered as causing offence to Muslims. One individual in particular has become renowned for his verbal attacks on Islam. Zakariya Butrus is not formally associated with the Coptic Orthodox Church but wears priestly garments during his programme, thus strengthening the belief in Egypt that al-Hayat is an anti-Islamic, pro-Coptic station.[35]

However, there has been recent interest from various sectors of the Coptic community in having their own satellite channel. Although there has been increased coverage of Coptic religious celebrations on Egyptian state-owned television, this is deemed insufficient. Furthermore, Copts argue that as Islamic channels are broadcasting about religion, and Christian-based stations are doing the same outside of Egypt, they should have the right to their own station. According to Bishop Musa, the dynamic Coptic Orthodox Bishop of Youth, it is vital that Egyptian Christians use the latest technology to minister to young people. 'We have a motto that if we are not on air, we are not on earth.'[36] The quest for a satellite channel, then, can be seen merely as a continuation of their tradition of having their own media (e.g, the church magazine *al-Keraza* and the Coptic-owned newspaper *Watani*).[37] The Coptic Orthodox Church has established a channel called *Agaphy* which broadcasts religious material, including the liturgy, Coptic language tuition, Bible studies and children's activities. Programmes are normally shot in churches and houses. Broadcasting since November 2005, the audience has initially been limited to the diaspora in the United States, partly as it has been funded primarily through private donations from the diaspora. In this way, *Agaphy* differs from the normal pattern, as it is not financed by a wealthy benefactor. While this is only one of several projects being launched by the church authorities, it is an indication of the importance placed by the church on providing the community abroad with religious education and, as a consequence, reaffirming their religious identity and maintaining contact with them.

It would appear that expatriate groups are not content with solely providing donations for church-owned satellite channels. At an expatriate conference entitled 'The Coptic Movement: A New Approach, Reality and Avenues' hosted by the Coptic Assembly of America in Chicago in October 2007, it was suggested that the expatriate community should establish a Coptic satellite channel.[38] Various figures who are well known in the activist circle are reported to have shown an interest. Based on public statements they have made on the Coptic situation, it would be expected that such a channel would raise politically sensitive issues as well as provide programmes on the Coptic faith and culture. Consequently, it would be difficult to obtain space on any satellite widely received in the Middle East. However, it is clear that this issue has the potential to have as much impact as the use of web technology has had on publicizing Coptic issues to a global audience.

The impact of the 'new media' on communal relations in Egypt
The stated aim of the émigré organizations is to safeguard Coptic rights. Yet, ironically, their activities can actually endanger the very community they are striving to protect. Expatriate groups have attracted adverse media attention in Egypt, partly due to their association with the West, notably the United States. As there have been few (if any) attempts by the groups to distance themselves from the US, this has led to the questioning of Coptic loyalty. Copts repeatedly stress their patriotism when in Egypt, but once they emigrate there is a perception that they are more willing to criticize their homeland. The émigré groups are regarded as capitalizing on tragic events with the intention of escalating

the situation in order to achieve their objective of attaining foreign intervention in Egyptian politics. Their frequent demands that the US should reduce the amount of financial aid given to Egypt serve only to provide evidence for the above suspicions. The Egyptian elite has always argued that any specific Coptic concerns must be dealt with as part of a general solution to problems affecting all Egyptians and consequently reject any deviation from this approach. For example, at the height of the tension over the International Religious Freedom Act, Osama al-Baz, political advisor to President Mubarak, warned that the US had no right to intervene in Egyptian internal affairs and that Egyptian Christians were the first to refuse foreign interference.[39] Thus, there is a clear belief that the 'Coptic issue' is a domestic one and outside intervention would be seen as an infringement of state sovereignty. Considering the inherent hostility in the region towards US foreign policy in the Middle East, this connection between the Copts and the US has increased tension in Egypt.

This environment also allows rumours circulated in the Egyptian press about US–Coptic relations to gain credibility and has forced denials from the concerned parties. For example, a report in 2007 stated that the US funnelled part of its aid given to Egypt directly to the Coptic community as part of its policy to 'empower' religious minorities and create divisions in the Arab world. In reality, some Christian non-governmental organizations are partners with USAID but receive funds to deliver socio-economic projects for both Muslims and Christians. Nevertheless, this story gained widespread coverage, to the extent that the Coptic Orthodox Church was forced to publicly deny that it received donations from the US government.[40] Similarly, discussions regarding the establishment of a Coptic satellite channel triggered mass debate. A notable Coptic intellectual argued that religious satellite channels would probably increase differences between the two communities when what was needed was an initiative to defuse communal tension.[41] Once more, the Coptic Orthodox Church was linked to the expatriate project, with headlines such as 'Expatriate Copts negotiate with Pope Shenouda to launch a satellite channel'.[42] In response, Bishop Marqus, a prominent figure within the hierarchy, declared that: 'The church opposed broadcasting issues via media that work on the spread of the spirit of enmity and extremism.'[43] These two examples are merely illustrations of the current environment in Egypt concerning communal relations. While there are obviously long-standing Coptic concerns that have not been fully addressed and that contribute to communal unrest, it is apparent that expatriate activities also contribute to this instability.

The Coptic community in Egypt has also been forced to respond to the campaigns launched by activists in the diaspora. For example, over 2,000 prominent Coptic figures in Egypt signed a petition denouncing the International Religious Freedom Act as 'continuing attempts' by a hostile enemy to spread 'false claims' of Coptic repression.[44] Yet it must also be noted that some members of the Coptic community in Egypt are supportive of the work carried out by the groups, especially the website publicity given to incidents that are often ignored in the Egyptian media with the exception of *Watani* newspaper. In this sense, they perceive that international interest in their situation both acts as protection against a deterioration in conditions and also helps to boost morale. Information is sent out of Egypt, especially photographs of incidents, while the wider community is kept informed of the organizations' campaigns abroad. In this way, Brinkerhoff suggests that the expatriate groups could potentially create 'accountable mechanisms'.[45] Furthermore, this fusion between the inside and outside is considered by Rowe to lend 'a credible air of authenticity to the movement'.[46]

This dilemma concerning support of the expatriate groups has also caused difficulties for the Coptic Orthodox Church, personified by Patriarch Shenouda. The patriarch has frequently stressed that these activists make up a small proportion of the Coptic diaspora and are not representative of the Church or the wider Coptic community. He has remained adamant that the Church is against foreign intervention in any Coptic issue, rejects the use of the term 'persecution', and emphasizes that Coptic concerns can only be solved through home-grown reforms.[47] He has also appealed directly to Coptic émigrés to retain pride in their Egyptian roots, visit Egypt, have personal experience of Christian–Muslim relations in today's Egypt, and become active in expatriate groups that promote the Egyptian national interest, not concerns exclusive to Copts.[48] Yet there is some ambivalence in the relationship between the Church and the émigré groups. The Church is not a monolithic institution and members, including the clergy, do contact the lobby groups. The patriarch rarely acts against these individuals, or indeed against those who are active in the diaspora. He claims that, as patriarch, he is the 'father of all Copts' and this will not be altered because of political beliefs. Furthermore, the Church is also reliant on financial contributions from the diaspora, thus softening criticism from the patriarch. Consequently, the patriarch is content to condemn actions that are likely to have an adverse effect on communal relations in Egypt without necessarily distancing himself from the individual activists.

A further complication in the relationship between the patriarch and the émigré groups is that the latter can be regarded as potential rivals to the position of the patriarch as spokesman and representative of the Coptic community to the government. Under this version of the *millet*, there are few credible alternatives to the political role of the patriarch.[49] However, as this system depends on the ability of the patriarch to co-opt his community, the presence of an independent actor in the shape of a diaspora community that affects the political agenda in Egypt has the potential to challenge this status quo. In an attempt to pre-empt this, the church under Patriarch Shenouda has focused on consolidating its strength in the diaspora in order to try to replicate its dominant situation in Egypt. While this has involved the establishment of a physical presence through the building of churches, creation of dioceses, annual patriarchal visits to the US, etc., the Church has also acknowledged the importance of virtual technology. Thus, the Coptic Orthodox Church has a significant online presence, including a patriarchal website (in Arabic and English) as well as sites related to specific dioceses.[50] These allow adherents abroad to participate in Church activities, download the weekly sermons given by the patriarch and read *al-Keraza*, the official Church magazine. As explored earlier, the Church is also venturing into the satellite television market, which at present is concentrated solely on the diaspora. Thus, one of the most ancient Christian Churches has embraced contemporary information and communications technology, partly to minister to its members as befits a modern and global Church in the twenty-first century but also in order to compete with potential rivals. The Church policy is to avoid divisions between the Church in the homeland and diaspora by focusing on the patriarch as a unifying figure who – just like modern technology – transcends borders. By preserving the Coptic identity and heritage in the diaspora, through this new media, the Church hopes to maintain its role in Egypt as the undisputed leader of the Coptic community.

Conclusion

This chapter has sought to expand the research field on 'new media' to include a specific subtype of non-state actor – the diaspora. By using the Coptic community as a case study, it is clear that both Internet technology and satellite television offer opportunities for the diaspora to become active in homeland politics. The by-products of globalization have encouraged multiple identities and allowed cultural identity to remain relevant in the diaspora. The Coptic model indicates that diaspora groups will attempt to use this technology to publicize their own interpretation of events affecting their community. In particular, they are willing to lobby host governments to intervene in what can be regarded as a domestic issue, thus posing a challenge to the principle of state sovereignty. Clearly, this leads to a mixed reaction in the homeland.

The Coptic community is presented with a dilemma: by internationalizing their situation and disseminating information about incidents in Egypt through their websites, the diaspora groups have attained Western attention. Yet this achievement has paradoxically been the cause of increased tension between Christians and Muslims in Egypt. The age-old Coptic balancing act of proving that they are patriotic Egyptians while retaining a strong attachment to their religious and cultural identity has become harder in the globalization era, when specific individuals and groups based on another continent can affect the domestic political environment. While it is important not to overestimate the power of the Coptic diaspora lobby, both in the host and homeland societies, it is clear that in the twenty-first century it is one further factor to consider when addressing communal relations in Egypt. Yet this use of technology has not been one-way. The Coptic Orthodox Church has used the same aspects of globalization in its aim to maintain its predominant position in Church–State relations in Egypt. Hence, both groups are using the new media to reach out to the other constituency in a contest that has the long-term potential not only to cause divisions within the Coptic community but also to further heighten tension between the Egyptian state, Muslim public and their Christian compatriots.

Without the interactive and instant characteristics of the Internet and satellite television, it is unlikely that the activities of the diaspora, or indeed the Coptic Orthodox Church, would have such resonance outside of their territorial bases. Therefore, this case study demonstrates the complex relationship between information and communications technology and the growth of diaspora involvement in homeland politics, indicating that governing authorities are unlikely to respond positively to this new challenge. This is unlikely to change if the diaspora continues to claim that it acts on behalf of a group with specific features that distinguish it from the majority population. Yet, as has been argued throughout the debate on the impact of globalization, it is clear that this particular aspect has both positive and negative effects on the Copts, serving to help unite the global Coptic community while simultaneously accentuating divisions in the homeland.

NOTES

1 Augustus Richard Norton, 'The New Media, Civic Pluralism and the Struggle for Political Reform', in Dale F. Eickelman and Jon W. Anderson (eds), *New Media in the Muslim World: The Emerging Public Sphere*, Bloomington: Indiana University Press, 2003, p. 22.
2 For further discussion, see the following: Emma C. Murphy, 'Agency and Space: The Political Impact of Information Technologies in the Gulf Arab States', *Third World Quarterly* 27, 2006, pp. 1059–83; Naomi Sakr, *Satellite Realms: Transnational Television, Globalization & the Middle East*, London: I.B. Tauris, 2001; and Mamoun Fandy, 'Information Technology, Trust, and Social Change in the Arab World', *Middle East Journal* 54, 2000, pp. 378–94.
3 Jan Aart Scholte, 'The Globalization of World Politics', in John Baylis and Steve Smith (eds), *The Globalization of World Politics*, Oxford: Oxford University Press, 2001, pp. 14–15.
4 Peter G. Mandaville, 'Reimagining the Ummah? Information Technology and the Changing Boundaries of Political Islam', in Ali Mohammadi (ed.), *Islam Encountering Globalization*, London: Routledge, 2002, p. 69.
5 Roland Robertson, *Globalization: Social Theory and Global Culture*, London: SAGE Publications, 1992, p. 102.
6 See Gabriel Sheffer, *Diaspora Politics: At Home Abroad*, Cambridge, UK: Cambridge University Press, 2003; Nicholas van Hear, *New Diasporas: The Mass Exodus, Dispersal and Regrouping of Migrant Communities*, London: UCL Press, 1998; and Steven Vertovec, *Religion and Diaspora* (Transnational Communities Working Paper Series), Oxford: University of Oxford, 2001.
7 Nicholas van Hear, *New Diasporas*, pp. 5–6
8 William Safran, 'Diasporas in Modern Societies: Myths of Homeland and Return', in Steven Vertovec and Robin Cohen (eds), *Migration, Diasporas and Transnationalism*, Cheltenham: Edward Elgar Publishing, 1999, pp. 364–5.
9 Aziz Atiya, *A History of Eastern Christianity*, London: Methuen & Co., 1968, p. 16.

10 For a historical account of the Coptic community, see Theodore Hall Partrick, *Traditional Eastern Christianity: A History of the Coptic Orthodox Church*, Greensboro: Fisher Park Press, 1996.
11 Christophe Asad, *Geopolitique de l'Egypte*, Bruxelles: Editions Complexe, 2002, p. 54.
12 For detailed accounts on the Coptic community today, see John H. Watson, *Among the Copts*, Brighton: Sussex Academic Press, 2000; Otto F. A. Meinardus, *Christians in Egypt: Orthodox, Catholic, and Protestant Communities Past and Present*, Cairo: The American University in Cairo Press, 2006; and Fiona McCallum, 'Desert Roots and Global Branches: The Journey of the Coptic Orthodox Church', *The Bulletin of the Royal Institute for Inter-Faith Studies* 7, 2005, pp. 69–97.
13 The *millet* system refers to the Ottoman method of dealing with religious groups as a collective rather than individuals. Paul Rowe describes its modern incarnation as a corporatist partnership between the Church and State. For more information, see Paul S. Rowe, 'Neo-millet Systems and Transnational Religious Movements: The Humayun Decrees and Church Construction in Egypt', *Journal of Church and State* 49, 2007, pp. 329–32.
14 For further details on the political concerns of the Coptic community today, see Fiona McCallum, 'Muslim–Christian Relations in Egypt: Challenges for the Twenty-first Century', in Anthony O'Mahony and Emma Loosley (eds), *Christian Responses to Islam: Muslim–Christian Relations in the Modern World*, Manchester: Manchester University Press, 2008.
15 For further information on Eastern Orthodox Christian communities in the United States, see Alexei D. Krindatch, 'Orthodox (Eastern Churches) in the United States at the Beginning of a New Millennium: Questions of Nature, Identity and Mission', *Journal for the Scientific Study of Religion* 41, 2002, pp. 533–63.
16 For a detailed account of the clash between Sadat and Shenouda, consult Nadia Ramsis Farah, *Religious Strife in Egypt: Crisis and Ideological Conflict in the Seventies*, London: Gordon and Breach Science Publishers, 1986.
17 See www.state.gov/g/drl/rls/irf, and Allen D. Hertzke and Daniel Philpott, 'Defending the Faiths', *National Interest* 61, 2000, pp. 74–81.
18 Consult the following websites for information about these groups: US Copts Association, www.copts.com; Middle East Christians Association, http://meca-humanrights.com/en/index.asp; American Coptic Association, www.amcoptic.com; Copts United, www.coptsunited.com. For an original approach on the role of the US Copts Association, see Jennifer M. Brinkerhoff, 'Digital Diasporas and Governance in Semi-Authoritarian States: The Case of the Egyptian Copts', *Public Administration and Development* 25, 2005, pp. 193–204.
19 US Copts Association, www.copts.com/english1/index.php/mission-statment/; accessed 18 February 2008.
20 See US Copts Association, www.copts.com.
21 See the Center for Arab West Understanding, www.arabwestreport.info.
22 Cornelis Hulsman, 'Christian Activists' Contributions to Christian Migration from the Arab World: Can Christianity Survive in the Arab World?', *Arab West Report*, 5 December 2007, www.arabwestreport.info; accessed 25 February 2008.

23 For a detailed discussion on church-building legislation in Egypt, see Paul S. Rowe, 'Neo-millet Systems and Transnational Religious Movements: The Humayun Decrees and Church Construction in Egypt' *Journal of Church and State* 49, 2007, pp. 334–42.
24 *The Economist*, 'Egypt's vulnerable Copts', 6 January 2000, www.economist.com /PrinterFriendly.cfm?Story_ID=271592; accessed 25 August 2003. See also Hulsman, 'Christian Activists' Contributions to Christian Migration from the Arab World'; accessed 25 February 2008.
25 BBC News, 'More arrests after Egypt clashes', 8 January 2000, http://news.bbc.co.uk/hi/world/middle_east/595716.stm; accessed 25 August 2003.
26 US Copts Association, 'The Egyptian Regime Encourages Persecution of Coptic Christians', 7 March 2002, www.copts.net/print.asp3id=272; accessed 10 October 2002.
27 Jennifer M. Brinkerhoff, 'Digital Diasporas and Governance in Semi-Authoritarian States: The Case of the Egyptian Copts', *Public Administration and Development* 25, 2005, p. 200.
28 Middle East Christians Association, http://meca-humanrights.com/en/index.asp; accessed 18 February 2008.
29 For example, Naomi Sakr, *Satellite Realms: Transnational Television, Globalization & the Middle East*, London: I.B. Tauris, 2001; Hugh Miles, *Al-Jazeera: How Arab TV News Challenged the World*, London: Abacus, 2005; Mohamed Zayani (ed.), *The al-Jazeera Phenomenon: Critical Perspectives on New Arab Media*, London: Pluto Press, 2005.
30 Naomi Sakr, *Satellite Realms*, pp. 61–5.
31 Edmund Ghareeb, 'New Media and the Information Revolution in the Arab World: An Assessment', *Middle East Journal* 54, 2000, p. 16.
32 Naomi Sakr, *Satellite Realms*, p. 61.
33 Reem Nafie, 'Many wary of faith-based TV', *al-Ahram Weekly*, http://weekly.ahram.org.eg/print/2005/769/eg11.htm; accessed 17 November 2005.
34 See *al-Hayat* Television, www.lifetv.tv.
35 See various articles in *Arab West Report* including Lotus Kiwan, 'Archpriest Zakariya Butrus', *Sawt al-Ummah*, 26 November 2007, available on Arab West Report, www.arabwestreport.info; accessed 19 February 2008.
36 Bishop Musa in Vivian Salama, 'The Love Network: New Coptic TV Channel "Agaphy" Hits the Airwaves', *Transnational Broadcasting Studies* 15, 2005, http://www,tbsjounrla.com/SalamaCopticPF.html; accessed 19 February 2008.
37 Vivian Salama, 'The Love Network'; accessed 19 February 2008.
38 *Arab West Report*, 'Press Review on the Coptic Assembly of America, the Chicago Conference', 24 October 2007, www.arabwestreport.info; accessed 24 January 2008.
39 Arabic News.com, 'El-Baz: US has no right to ask Egypt about Copts' situation', 7 October 1998, www.arabicnews.com/ansub/Daily/Day/980710/1998071064.html; accessed 27 August 2003.
40 For further information, see Emad Mekay, 'Empowering the Copts', *al-Ahram Weekly*, http://weekly.ahram.org.eg/print/2007/858/fr2.htm; accessed 20 August 2007.
41 Reem Nafie, 'Many wary of faith-based TV', *al-Ahram Weekly*, 17 November 2005, http://weekly.ahram.org.eg/print/2005/769/eg11.htm; accessed 17 November 2005.

42 Michael Adil, 'Expatriate Copts negotiate with Pope Shenouda to launch a satellite channel from Egypt', *Rose al-Yusuf*, 30 October 2007; available on *Arab West Report*, www.arabwestreport.info; accessed 24 January 2008.
43 Michael Adil, 'Bishop Marqus: The church has no relation with Abadir's channel', *Rose al-Yusuf*, 2 December 2007; available on *Arab West Report*, www.arabwestreport.info; accessed 19 February 2008.
44 Arabic News.com, 'Pope Shenouda highlights Egypt's religious tolerance, improvements needed', 31 May 2002, http://www.arabicnewx.com/ansub/Daily/Day/020531/2002053135.html; accessed 27 August 2003.
45 Jennifer M. Brinkerhoff, 'Digital Diasporas and Governance in Semi-Authoritarian States, pp. 199–201.
46 Paul S. Rowe, 'Four Guys and a Fax Machine? Diasporas, New Information Technologies, and the Internationalization of Religion in Egypt', *Journal of Church and State* 43, 2001, p. 91.
47 Arabic News.com, 'On the Coptic issue in Egypt', 6 November 1998, http://www.arabicnewx.com/ansub/Daily/Day/981106/1998110620.html; accessed 27 August 2003.
48 Arabic News.com, 'On the Coptic issue in Egypt'; accessed 27 August 2003.
49 For further discussion on the political role of the Coptic Orthodox Patriarch, see Fiona McCallum, 'The Political Role of the Patriarch in the Contemporary Middle East', *Middle Eastern Studies* 43, 2007, pp. 923–40.
50 See the Coptic Orthodox Patriarch website: www.copticpope.org.

7

Between Image and Reality:
New ICTs and the Arab Public Sphere

Emma Murphy

Introduction

The introduction of satellite television, the Internet and mobile telephone technology to the Arab world over the last two decades has opened up debates as to whether there is an identifiable public sphere emerging in the region. On first examination, it is difficult to see how a concept developed by a German philosopher to explain the emergence of political discourse in Europe during the periods of mercantile and early industrial capitalism is readily applicable to the twenty-first century Middle East. However, as this chapter hopes to show, it has offered political analysts a useful tool for determining the nature, extent and impact of new forms of political communication that have the potential to alter existing state–society relations in favour of more liberal and citizen-friendly arrangements. Whether that potential has actually been realized is a different question and one to which there remains no conclusive answer as yet. Evidence does suggest, however, that the combined efforts of agents ranging from local regime elites, government bureaucracies, global corporate entities and media formations have served as much to limit the emancipatory possibilities offered by the new technologies as to explore them.

However, it can be argued that the *appearance* of political contestation that the new media technologies allow is itself important, possessing a symbolic power and altering the frame for political discourse in crucial ways that may not necessarily amount to direct political challenges to the state but that nonetheless impinge upon its ability to resist new forms of political action. The danger of such a symbolic role is the possibility that society surrenders to the spectacular, and to the colonizing attributes of informational capitalism. In this scenario, the state becomes the agent of global capitalist forces and challenges to it are both illusory and irrelevant.

The chapter explores the tensions between these two alternative understandings of how contemporary media-based ICTs are impacting upon state–society relations, suggesting that there exists a dialectical reciprocity between the image and reality of a public sphere that is itself the potential source for political change in the Arab world.

The Habermasian public sphere

Habermas' original exposition on the public sphere was published in 1962 under the title *Strukturwandel der Öffenlicheit*. It was a historical-sociological account of the emergence, transformation and ultimate demise of a political space in which civil society embarked on a critical discussion of matters of general public interest, thereby posing a challenge to the prevailing state authorities as to how they managed and met those public interests. Through informed and critical discussion, the public forced the state authorities into accountability. This was a specifically European phenomenon, which arose from the emergence of increasingly autonomous professional (or bourgeois) classes out of the mercantile and then industrial revolutions. This bourgeois class attained, along with literacy and the commercially driven imperative of communicating news and information ever more widely and speedily, a new political self-consciousness, which manifested itself in newspapers, reading societies and political salons. The arena of debate, the *public sphere*, was inherently liberal, rational and virtuous, insofar as it included a normative commitment to the equality of participants. As time progressed, however, news itself became commodified by rising capitalism. The press became commercialized; it ceased to be autonomous as it incorporated ideological position, pandered to popular opinion or party politics, and became increasingly reliant on advertising revenues to sustain its increasingly profit-oriented motivation (epitomized by the editorial function). By the twentieth century, this idealized arena in which public opinion was formed and contested began to diminish under the weight of self-interested capitalist intrusion. Private capital had invaded the public sphere, impeding the freedom and rationalism of debate. The state, meanwhile, has also begun to utilize the media in its efforts to engage and negotiate with interest groups, notably the socially and economically deprived. The transformation of the Liberal Constitutional State into the Social Welfare State signalled further blurring of the lines between public and private domains. State–society negotiation no longer took place through public disinterested discussions but rather through institutional and fundamentally interested arrangements. The bourgeois public sphere was thus penetrated and subordinated to the point of its demise.

Media-based ICTs and the public sphere in the Arab world

So how does this historically and geographically specific, not to mention highly idealized, public sphere help us to unravel what is currently taking place in the Arab world? The Arab world did not follow a comparable developmental route to Europe and has no obvious parallel experience of liberal public debate. Capitalism was introduced by imperialist European powers, and the post-independence Arab states have struggled ever since to counter the disadvantages of the subsequent structural impediments to development and the problems of late development in general. If anything, the region has been characterized by the absence of an autonomous industrial bourgeoisie[1] that could kick-start critical scrutiny of the state, while the state appropriation of the means for mass communication was a cornerstone of modernization strategies in the postcolonial period. The combined consequences of state media monopolies, corporatist political structures and military-backed elites were, until recently, an absence of free debate, profoundly embedded censorship regimes and an unidentifiable Arab public, either regionally or – with the exception perhaps of Lebanon – at the local level.

That is not to suggest that a public has not existed in the Arab world. Indeed, the nineteenth and early twentieth centuries witnessed the growth of a largely bourgeois public that did indeed debate questions of identity and modernity within the context of Islam and the Arab world's responses to Ottoman decline, Turkish ascendance and – latterly – European rule. This debate took place first within literary and intellectual salons, and then through printed news media and pamphleting. However, the limited literacy among Arab populations, and the technical constraints on communications, meant that debate was confined to an often Western-educated elite who frequently and ironically used both the languages and discourses of Europe to articulate their emerging and self-conscious concerns. The struggle for independence, the essentializing and totalizing impact of Arab nationalism, and the subsequent structural impediments imposed by corporatist politics, combined to suppress even this public in the second half of the twentieth century. The single voice of the state came to dominate public conversations, determining its parameters and contours while shrouding alternative voices through its repressive coercive and discursive powers.

Arguably, the so-called *new* media, principally satellite television, the Internet and GSM telephonic technology, have explosively shattered this paradigm. Satellite television made its debut in the Arab world, at least at the mass level, when Saudi Arabia began installing hardware close to the Iraqi border in 1991, allowing the American channel, CNN, to be downloaded and re-broadcast via terrestrial means. Simultaneously, the Egyptian company, ESN, took a position in a European satellite that allowed it to broadcast across the region. Since then, there has been a rapid proliferation of Arab-owned satellite television companies and channels, offering Arabic-language programming that is accessible to Arabs regardless of their country of residence. The headline-grabbing, Qatari-owned al-Jazeera has been at the forefront of a new trend in socially and politically critical taboo-breaking coverage. But, more generally, there has been a revolution in the way in which television formats are constructed and their messaging compiled, which has included state-owned terrestrial channels that are now forced to compete with their popular and professionalized satellite counterparts. The new satellite companies have introduced private ownership into delivery of television programming, eroding state monopolies and forcing a new regulatory agenda to replace the old.

The Internet also made its way into the Arab region in the early 1990s, although usage is still limited in global terms and unevenly distributed between and within Arab countries. The key point, however, is the rate at which Internet usage is now growing: between 2000 and 2007, usage in the Middle East region had reportedly grown by 920 per cent (compared with 221.5 per cent in Europe and 117.2 per cent in North America).[2] Levels of penetration vary from 42.9 per cent of the population in the UAE to just 1.3 per cent in Yemen and 0.1 per cent in Iraq (although the statistics available should be treated with caution as they rely on reported subscription rates and PCs per household and thus exclude many actual users who access the Internet via cyber cafes, universities and other facilities). The last decade in particular has seen a rapid increase in the amount of web material available in the Arabic language, and a proliferation of intermediary companies that translate software and utilities into Arabic for local usage. Despite its latecomer status, the Arab region is undoubtedly now online.

Simultaneously, GSM technology has allowed mobile telephones to become an indispensable accessory. Mobile telephone markets have been opened to private and even foreign investment, resulting in impressive sectoral growth. By the end of 2005 there were 33 mobile operators in the Arab world, and in 2008 the last market (Qatar) was opened to competition. GSM subscriber rates in 2005 varied from 102.99 per cent of the population in Bahrain, 100.86 per cent in the UAE and 92.15 per cent in Qatar to 9.54 per cent in Yemen, 5.48 per cent in Sudan and 4.15 per cent in Libya.[3] Even the state-owned companies have been partially privatized, although their commitment to the more expensive task of fixed-line investment means that they retain a strategic function and a dominant market role in that area.

It is clear that the ICT revolution has made a substantial impact upon media and communications provision in the Arab world, the single biggest component of which is the erosion of state monopolies on the ownership and content of mass communications systems. The private sector, entrepreneurial capital, is playing a major role as the engine for development in the sector. Furthermore, efforts by the state to control the content of communications have become substantially more hampered, with territorial borders growing progressively less relevant in terms of access to means of communication and the delivery of messages. In this context, it is hardly surprising that journalists, academics, oppositionists and activists alike have proclaimed a new era of communicative action in which civil society can evade the censorial compulsions of the Arab state to engage in reasoned, oppositional and critical debate. In this new virtual political space, it has been suggested that civil society can develop autonomously from state controls, define its interests and agendas through debate, and then project them back onto the authoritarian state in the form of critical scrutiny. The terms *public*, *public opinion* and *public sphere* have thus gained new currency, although there is no consensus on the degree to which any or all of them exist, if indeed they do.

The argument that a new *public* exists rests on the extent of popular engagement with the technologies. Jon Anderson[4] (addressing the broader Muslim world) has highlighted the range and number of interpreters of information, the falling away of barriers to entry to discursive arenas and the opportunities for increased dissemination of messages through their migration between technologies. The authority of messaging is more diffuse and popularized, amounting perhaps to the democratization of the informational realm not unlike the horizontally structured network society of Manuel Castells.[5] Participation in informational circuits is certainly more accessible today: the Arab citizen does not have to be literate to access political debates formerly confined to the print media and banned from state-run television but now regularly aired by satellite channels; he or she can express an opinion through telephone and text voting on the issues raised, votes that are unimpeded by disruptive agencies like the state. Programming is far more diverse, reflecting multiple, including minority, identities. Of course, as Noha Mellor[6] has pointed out, this fragments a public even as it seeks to be inclusive. Access remains limited by geography, ability to pay and pre-existing skills like language. The new technologies can reinforce existing social differentiation by exhibiting messages that are non-unitary and share only their discursive function. Much as Nancy Fraser suggested in her own critique of Habermas, the public sphere is the domain of many publics rather than one. The bourgeois public sphere, for all its purported virtue, was exclusivist. The voices of socially subordinate or marginalized elements, not least of which were those of women, were not given access and thus were forced into alternative discursive arenas. These multiple *subaltern counter publics* were equally not necessarily virtuous or inclusivist themselves. Nonetheless, as Habermas responded, in simply existing and voicing their challenges to the hegemony of the bourgeoisie over the public sphere, they contributed to the vitality of discussion needed to enhance the political project. Thus the diversity of messengers and messages suggests an evolving public or publics, but is not evidence of a fully functioning public sphere in the Habermasian sense.

One could argue that evidence of a public sphere can be found in the translation of the debate and discourse facilitated by the new technologies into political action and direct political contest between civil society and the state. It is not sufficient for a public to simply 'be'; it must visibly take action (communicative action) to prove its own existence and fulfil its function. Lina Khatib's work on the Beirut Spring suggests that the new media can indeed serve as a means for mobilizing and directing political action that contests the arbitrary power of the state,[7] although her assertion that this democratic public sphere was 'short-lived' echoes some of the assessments of new media generally that they create transient interest-based communities[8] rather than the embedded identity-based communities that fostered the public and counter-publics of the Habermasian public sphere.[9] Alternatively, Marc Lynch[10] argues that a new self-consciously *Arab* public is emerging that spans the region and that frequently 'trumps' the pre-existing, albeit limited, public spheres of individual states.

This new public emerged in something of a cocoon, with a sharp contrast between its internally extraordinarily public politics and its general isolation from wider international debates and concerns. Its arguments took place within a common frame of reference: an Arab identity discourse that shaped and inflected all arguments, analysis and coverage. Together, these three elements produced a distinctive kind of public sphere: an identity-bounded enclave, internally open but externally opaque.[11]

The problem, as Lynch himself identifies, is determining whether this form of public sphere can fulfil the Habermasian function of critical review and serve as a foundation for political reform and liberalization in a region where authoritarian states show little inclination to surrender power willingly.

Limits to the public sphere(s) in the Arab world

Thus, if we accept the arguments of Khatib, Lynch and others[12] that there exists one or more publics in the Arab World, we have to acknowledge their uniqueness and limitations. For a start, if the new publics created by the new media are not confined to nation states, then in what ways can they challenge the inadequacies of national regimes? Do the discourses of reform, liberalism, democracy or even – given that counter-publics need not themselves be virtuous – Islamist exclusivism need to be targeted at specific authorities and institutions in order to have the required critical effect? Lynch himself has acknowledged that this new Arab public has no corresponding executive or legislative institution to act on the consensus that might be formulated within its sphere. It could be argued, however, that the Habermasian notion of communicative action needs to be adjusted in the era of the non-territorially defined and segmented global village of Castells. Jodi Dean et al.[13] have argued convincingly that in this context we need to change the way we think about democratic imagery, popular participation, accountability and legitimacy; to move away from simple binaries of freedom and coercion, state and society. Instead of viewing the technology itself as just a tool to facilitate change in established systems within a given country, we need to focus on how the technology alters social relations themselves, producing new and unpredictable 'assemblages of power' that have little to do with national governments. New forms of political activism that utilize less direct techniques of leading, directing, opposing and controlling become necessary and possible. They draw upon Foucault's concept of governmentality, which articulates a particular kind of political knowledge: knowledge as part of the practice, systematization and rationalization of the field to be governed. The agency in this activity is less likely to be the individual or an elected body and more likely to be an interest-based civil society organization that uses ICTs to 'challenge previous configurations of power and influence and produce new ones'. The objectives of activism are not (solely) tied to offering a rational critique of the state and its policies (although they might include this) but are more diverse, less politically tangible, and not necessarily rational. Alternatively, one can argue, as Dean et al. have acknowledged, that in this world in which the relevance of the national community is subordinated to transnational political activism, the direct accountability of individual state authorities is diminished, while simultaneously unequal access to new technologies translates into new, hidden hierarchies of power.

To put it crudely, the *appearance* of having a critical public debate is not always matched by its reality. An example might be found in Imad Karam's study of Arab youth and satellite television. On the basis of focus-group investigations, Karam argues that, while satellite television has appeared to offer new, youth-oriented programmes that break with traditional media concentration on the concerns of the older generation, in fact the content of these programmes has remained determined by existing hierarchies. Young people are presumed to be almost exclusively interested in entertainment because their appetite for news and factual programming is low. But the youths interviewed for the research argued that the formats for news and factual programming remain constrained by frames that reflect the life experiences and prejudices of the older generation. Political programming concentrates on the negative aspects of life in the Arab world, offering few messages of hope for the young.

Thus they turn away from political programmes, even though they are not necessarily unpolitical. Similarly, programmes about youth are produced and presented by the older generation: the young Arabs themselves feel deprived of a voice and believe that their interests are poorly represented. So, even though a review of programming schedules might suggest programmes specifically addressing the interests of the young public, they are not themselves participant in the conversation.

A further example of this mismatch between appearances and reality has been offered by Mamoun Fandy. He has argued that the contemporary Arab media, for all its claims to offer free and critical debate, in fact remains inherently political and tied to the apron strings of informationally restrictive Arab states.[14] He cites as evidence the instrumentalist motivations behind the establishment of the Qatari-based al-Jazeera and the Saudi-owned al-Arabiya satellite channels. In his view, the editorial lines of these programmes, their unwillingness to criticize political elites at home even as they talk of the need for democratization elsewhere in the Arab world, have demonstrated that they are tools of national foreign policy rather than genuine efforts to open up the dialogical space.[15] His work brings into focus a crucial element of this public sphere, such as it is: its already diminished nature in terms of interested participation.

The truth is that the new media have never been disinterested – they are produced, reproduced, distributed, imported and embedded by the private sector, which operates to a profit motive and is fundamentally linked to global technology networks. Moreover, their capacity to introduce and embed the new media within the Arab region is closely dependent on ties with regime elites and state apparatuses. Even where the state has taken the initiative in setting policy agendas for technology-based development (such as in Tunisia, Jordan or Egypt), it has worked in partnership with, or been dependent on, technology-based private capital.

Naomi Sakr has provided evidence that Arab satellite channel ownership is concentrated in the hands of super-rich individuals, closely linked to regime elites (particularly in Saudi Arabia) and thoroughly tied in to broader global capitalist networks.[16] These satellite channels remain tightly constrained by their partnership, however informal it may be, with authoritarian Arab states, leaders of which are themselves eager to realize the economic benefits of new media technologies but highly resistant to any liberalizing political messages. It is no coincidence that the Arab League adopted a new Arab media charter in 2008 that invites Arab broadcasters 'not to damage social harmony, national unity, public order or traditional virtues'.[17] The charter was initiated by Egypt and Saudi Arabia, the two countries wherein most satellite television ownership is located, and empowers governments to take 'necessary legislative measures to deal with violations'. It is much like a gentleman's agreement whereby Arab regimes agree not to interfere in each other's efforts to reign in the critical dimensions of the new media-based public sphere. The Arab state is enacting a resourceful and determined fightback. Strategies are both direct (censorship, compulsory filtering of websites, arresting and imprisoning critical bloggers and webmasters, banning entire technologies) and indirect (controlling ISP licensing, co-opting capitalist media owners, encouraging nominally culturally based self-censorship, professionalizing its own media outlets to present stronger competition, and adopting the discourse of the free media in order to subvert its use by others).[18]

The fact that Arab regimes have been so proactive in their efforts to counter the effect of the new public sphere(s) suggests that such a sphere (or spheres) does indeed exist: if the governments think it poses a real challenge, then it must be a real challenge. Equally, however, the collaboration between private capital and state serves to seriously constrain its ability to function as a critical domain. The domination of interested parties – state and private capital – amounts to an early diminishment of a public space still in its infancy.

The public sphere as spectacle?

The above is not to argue that the appearance of the public(s) through the new media is not real but rather that it has dimensions and functions beyond the Habermasian ideal. One could argue, for example, that the appearance or *image* of a public is as important as the *reality* of a public. After all, as Jean Baudrillard suggested in *Simulations*, the media are not just vehicles for reporting events or reflecting reality; they are part of the conditions that create that reality. Moreover, they play a crucial role in determining how those events or acts are understood and responded to. The relationship between image and reality is inverted by the mediatory function of the media and, progressively, the distinction between simulation and reality is eroded. According to this logic, it does not matter whether the critical discourses of the public(s) aired by the new media *actually* have the capacity *in and of themselves* to mobilize direct contestation of the state; the mere fact the new media present the image of a critical public sphere is sufficient to create that capacity and force Arab regimes to respond. The state may fight back through its various strategies to put boundaries around the political spaces of the public sphere, and to some extent it may be able to do so. However, the dialectical relationship between image and reality means that, over time, the discursive context within which the state and its collaborative agents are operating is nonetheless changing in ways that challenge the role and actions of the state and that constantly serve both to test those boundaries and to make them less relevant.

However, it is not only the characteristics of the political discourse in the public sphere that matter. The new media in the Arab world has proliferated and mixed the messaging to which Arab populations are exposed in more than just the political domain. The homogenized social, religious and cultural messages associated with state-controlled media in contexts of nation-building have given way to a vast diversity of messages that are often profoundly at odds with those that preceded them and that have eroded the cultural boundaries that previously mapped onto their sovereign counterparts.

Lynch suggested that there remains a degree of protection for the Arab world from external publics, and this is true insofar as the Arabic language remains a primary message filter for the region. Elites and middle classes are able to access English-language information more readily than lower income groups but the old-style trust in English-language news sources above local state-managed Arabic sources is being eroded by a growing belief in the objectivity and professionalism of (some) Arab sources such as al-Jazeera. Similarly, messages reflecting Arab identities and interests remain under-represented in external public spheres. This is partly a result of the limited part played by Arab firms in the production and global reproduction of the technologies themselves, although some inroads are being made here by Arab Gulf mobile telephone companies. It is also because Arab messages are directed predominantly at Arabic–speaking audiences, either in the region or in global diasporas. While there were 315 satellite television channels servicing the Middle East in 2007, the penetration by Arab companies of non-Arab markets was severely restricted. Al-Jazeera is currently the only international brand satellite television company offering a fully English-language channel, although some of the North African stations like 2M Maroc or Tunis 7 offer mixed Arabic–French programming and many, such as al-Arabiya, offer English-language web pages. Al-Jazeera's package is qualitatively the most superior, including news services available globally via SMS, with the anticipated extension to MMS and even new landline services. For the most part, the global reach of Arab satellite companies amounts to free-to-air services in Arabic targeting Arab diaspora communities. In the USA, for example, there are currently 36 such channels. So, even if the Arab voice has a global reach, its audience remains linguistically defined and its role in a global public sphere constrained. The Internet, too, retains some structural impediments to diffusion of Arab messages, not least the subordinate status of Arabic as an Internet language. (In 2004 the United Nations declared that there were too few Arabic-language websites to even be statistically relevant![19]) The one area where this really might not be the case, although the empirical evidence is not sufficiently systematic to be sure, is in that of the Islamic public. The global character of this pubic, as opposed to the regionally and linguistically defined character of the Arab public, renders the possibilities greater for messages to be translated and made more universally available.

So much for the limited export of message, but what of imports? There can be little doubt that, partly as a result of the high costs of producing programmes locally, the Arab television media have increasingly resorted to importing programming and formats from (predominantly) the West. The popularity of *Pop Idol*-type talent shows, the import and mimicking of dramas and sitcoms (like the American show *Friends*), competitions like *Who Wants to be a Millionaire?*, and intense and combative interview formats, all indicate the progression of what is termed *cultural hybridity* or *global convergence*. Mellor calls this the 'regressive Americanization' of Arab media culture[20] and it can be manifested in more sinister forms than simply programme imports. In Qatar, for example, the newsprint media launched a campaign in 2007 to protest against the virtual absence of Qatari nations in either the editorial or presentational sides of al-Jazeera's operations. The station was accused of preferring Western news presenters and styles of dress, and even Arabs with Western facial features. The implication was that Western equated with a more modern, professional, objective and authoritative voice, while Qatari or Arab cultural presentations were less so. The styles, language, materials, values and presentational attributes of the West are seeping through the new media in the Arab world, just as much as the direct messaging. Even the increasingly fragmented programming – the 'something for everyone' approach that positions the Arabic version of *The Simpsons* (*Al Shamshoon*) next to a programme for Arab women (*Kalam Nazeam*), and that includes *Who Wants to Be a Millionaire?* with George Kurdahi's *Khawater Shab* (for young, Islamically minded Saudis) and *Danadana* (an Arab musical celebrity show) in the same day's MBC schedule – suggests a bombardment of mixed messaging within which political discourse and contestation is just one component.

In this context, the discursive political arena may be viewed as a commodity, as much as any of the other message formats. Private ownership leaves satellite television open to the pressures of revenue generation and thus to the advertising imperative. Oddly enough, there is as yet no trans-regional systematic collection of audience statistics, but it is clear that Saudi Arabia (as the richest regional market) sets the agenda by virtue of its advertising power. It is no coincidence that al-Jazeera – which has been sufficiently contestational as to be banned from operating at one time or another in pretty well every Arab state – remains reliant on the financial patronage of the Qatari emir. The channel has become a brand that represents (more) objective news coverage, open debate of once politically and socially taboo subjects, hard-hitting critiques of politics within the Arab world and a global view. When viewers tune in, are they purchasing the brand item or are they witnessing, or even participating in, a public sphere?

If one were to take the former to be the case, and the sole dimension to apparent political contestation via the new media, one would be in the realms of Guy Debord and the *Situationist International*. They argued that experience itself is commodified by the media and consumer culture and that we express ourselves by what we buy rather than by what we create. As Debord himself said: 'The spectacle corresponds to the historical moment at which the commodity completes its colonisation of social life.'[21] Our social and political relationships are mediated through images, managed by the producers of those images, and thus we become passive bystanders to our own lives. In other words, one could suggest that watching al-Jazeera identifies one as a politically aware Arab who is keen to see political issues debated in a lively way even though no actual political activity is required to sustain that identity. The act of debate is more *spectacle* than contest with the state – indeed, it actually substitutes for that contest by making believe that such a contest exists at all.

It is important to stress that this argument need not be confined to the physical imagery of television: apart from the fact that the various components of the new media are inextricably and organically interconnected (hence the easy message migration between media), the Internet in particular has its own attributes that suggest commodification. The Internet sustains an overwhelming quantity of information but no mechanism for ensuring its quality. Information is not the same as knowledge, and the inter-subjective, experiential nature of much of the information that it does support is not comparable to either real experience or authoritative interpretation.[22] Internet users must necessarily be selective in what they choose to access, and must be interpretive in the authority they attribute to it. They themselves are not neutral beings but are pre-shaped by their exposure to hegemonic discourses (to which they may consent or resist). They are consumers of a product, exercising choice on the basis of their social, political, cultural and economic pre-existence. The content of the messages that they choose to access comprises a commodity. Those sources of information that cannot place their goods on the Internet shelf have less power over the information market; those that can pay to place their product higher up the Google or Yahoo search engine's outpourings have greater market power. As Barney Warf and John Grimes aptly put it: 'Because the Net has metamorphosed into an office park, shopping mall, and entertainment arcade, it is sheer fantasy to expect that it will remain a libertarian island in a world of conflicting political objectives.'[23] The implication here is that the mere existence of messages of political contestation on the web does not necessarily constitute a functioning public sphere. Discursive websites have to be accessed in order to serve this function and there has to be some translation from access to action in order to equate with *public* as opposed to *private* opinion. Moreover, the existence of discursive websites has to be viewed within *the context* of consumer culture and global informational capitalism as a whole.

The evidence, however, suggests that it would be excessive to claim, as the Marxist sociologist Henri Lefebvre did for Europe,[24] that daily life in the Arab World has now been thoroughly *colonized* by capitalism, and that Arabs are entirely reduced by the modern media to the status of passive consumers. For a start, there remains a cultural resistance to the hegemonic assertion of informational capitalism embedded within the social fabric. Counter-hegemonic influences include Islamic social forces that seek to protect the Arab cultural domain from the evils of pornography, secularism, youthful disobedience and Western-style social breakdown. The Saudi *ulema* thus fought to prevent the local sale of camera phones that enable the circulation of pictures of uncovered women and unmonitored communication between the sexes. They were ultimately less successful than the Parent–Teachers Association in Dubai, the lobbies of which secured the installation of filters by the local ISP to prevent access to pornographic and other culturally offensive websites. Saudi advertisers meanwhile act as a filtering mechanism for the satellite television programmes they sponsor, serving to balance imported cultural influences through the provision of a fair dose of culturally authentic programming. In the Internet domain, there is no shortage of Islamic and Arab civil society activity, as well as individual blogging, which presents alternative cultural models to those of the global consumer of capitalist informational products. This counter-hegemonic resistance is both cultural and political in form, and is able to utilize the exclusivity of the Arabic language as a shield against penetration from the outside.

The Arab state itself is also working to resist its own subordination to global norms and regulatory regimes, as much as it is constantly seeking new ways to bend the embedding of new ICTs in the region to the developmental, rather than political, path. Tunisia, for example, played a leading role in efforts to transfer governance of the Internet to an international organization made up of governmental representatives (including itself, no doubt) and away from the current USA-based public–private partnership. In 2005 it hosted the second World Summit on the Information Society (WSIS), the more benign interpretation of which was that the Tunisian government was playing its part in the promotion of multiple stakeholder governance to include less developed countries of the world. Tunisia's critics, including its own beleaguered civil society organizations, suggested instead that the regime was seeking to co-opt the discourses of the information society, even as it imposed heavy censoring methods on non-state actors seeking to participate in the summit. The state in the Arab world is by no means out of the game here, but should be considered a live agent, with considerable means at its disposal to counter the efforts of global actors (capitalist or otherwise) to integrate the region in a free flow of knowledge and ideas. It is not alone in this! Indeed the WSIS process itself, in drawing the previously under-represented voices of developing countries into the debates over the globalization of the information society, has arguably promoted the opportunities for authoritarian self-assertion.

> Critics[,however,] have argued that the WSIS process reflects an attempt by some states operating through international organizations to assert government control over the Internet. They express concern that this could lead to censorship of content, limitations on on-line behaviour, stifling innovations, and, more generally, a reduction of the Internet's character as a free space of civil society, beyond social and geographic boundaries.[25]

The 2003 *Arab Human Development Report*[26] explicitly recognized the role played by the authoritarian Arab state as just one of a string of political and cultural impediments to a knowledge-based society. Apart from an unwillingness to tolerate free debate, and a tendency to use brutal means to stifle such debate when its strikes too close to home, the Arab state has (according to the report) overseen a declining quality of formal education and historically low levels of investment in research and development. In terms of the arguments presented above, this is a mixed blessing: on the one hand, the Arab world is more likely to be relegated to the role of consumer, rather than innovator, of informational products, while on the other hand it has been slower to make such consumption accessible to its wider populations and therefore to allow their subordination to the hegemonic aspirations of informational capitalism. In development terms, of course, it has the potential for disaster. The Arab state, meanwhile, plays a double game as, on the one hand, an agent that collaborates with global capitalism's media activities in order to maximize self-advantage for privileged elites and, on the other, a restrictive agent that seeks to control the inflow of influences that might challenge its local hegemonic position. Understanding this means deconstructing the state itself, recognizing the multiplicity of often contradictory interests that are embedded within it as well as the multiple functions served by the components of the state apparatus.

Finally, but perhaps most importantly, one cannot simply dismiss the proliferation of civil society activities via the new media technologies, merely because – as yet – they have not resulted in profoundly visible and sustained political change in specific national systems. Admittedly, they may be more transient and amorphous than the nationally based civil society organizations of the past. A Facebook-driven protest group lacks the tangible and lasting structures and processes of a trade union. Yet the blossoming of the Arab blogosphere, the often comic use of YouTube to anonymously circulate critical political messages and the global dissemination of competing Islamist discourses all serve to generate a new political environment in a way that we cannot yet fully comprehend or evaluate.

Indeed, the sum total of the discussion above is to suggest that, while a rigid application of the concept of a Habermasian public sphere is of limited utility in analyzing the role of the new media in the Arab World, the broader connotations of the concept nonetheless offer us a starting point for identifying and acknowledging an alternative and possibly regionally unique form of public sphere. In this, the emancipatory possibilities of the public sphere are no more important than its diminishment and colonization – the two processes being enacted simultaneously and through the agency of multiple actors, some of which may assume contradictory functions in and of themselves.

Conclusion: public spheres in the era of new media; what is Arab and what is not?

The first conclusion to which the discussion leads is generic and admittedly unoriginal: that technology is not itself culturally or politically neutral. The new media technologies contain biases within them that expand the domain of informational capital and its hegemonic cultural influences. Since these originate from outside the Arab world, then the introduction of such technologies to the region brings with it a subordinating and consumer-based reorientation and a tendency to reproduce spectacle rather than reality, a process that has already been experienced in the technology-originating societies. This process is at odds with the second characteristic of the new technologies: their capacity to offer new and freer political spaces in which political debate can take place and civil society can challenge the political status quo. Habermas suggested that the latter would inevitably succumb to the former in a sequential manner, while the Arab experience suggests that the two processes may occur simultaneously.

A second conclusion is that – in the era of mass communication and beyond the developmentalist state of the past – the image of a functioning public sphere may be as important as the reality; that the potential for actual political contestation and change lies in the dialectical reciprocity between the two. The state, no longer able to monopolize the technologies or the messages they convey, becomes just one of a number of agencies seeking to shape the messages through the ownership and regulation of the technologies, access to them, content within them and responses to them. How this competition is mediated and ultimately portrayed by the media themselves becomes a part of the story and an agency in and of itself.

A final conclusion, and one that offers perhaps a more positive note on which to end, is that the Arab world is still clearly in a transitional phase. It might have been a latecomer to the ICT revolution, but the pace of change is accelerating rapidly, driven primarily by private enterprise and social demand. The Arab state has cottoned on to the developmental (and security) benefits of ICTs, and is increasingly strategizing accordingly. But the agencies involved in reproducing, embedding and utilizing the technologies are multiple, and include among them civil society agencies committed to political contestation (be it virtuous or not). They have been able to draw upon local cultural and linguistic frames to filter out some of the less desirable (for them) impacts of ICT proliferation, even as they have drawn upon the attributes of the technologies themselves to develop new modes of political and communicative activism. They have collectively reframed the discourse itself, forcing regimes to respond to that, if nothing else. Where that process leads is yet to be seen.

NOTES

1 This argument has been made forcibly by writers such as Nazih Ayubi in *Over-stating the Arab State: Politics and Society in the Middle East*, London: I.B. Tauris, 2001.
2 Booz Allen Hamilton, 'The Impact of the ICT Sector on Economic Development in the Middle East', http://www.boozallencom/compabilities/Industries/industries_article; accessed 6 June 2007.
3 Zaywa, 'Top Arab Companies', http://www.zaywa.com/story.cfm/sidZAYWA 20051213122619; accessed 6 March 2008.
4 Jon Anderson, 'New Media in the Muslim World: The Emerging Public Sphere', *ISIM Newsletter*, No. 5, 2000.
5 Manuel Castells, *The Information Age: Economy, Society and* Culture, 3 vols, Oxford: Blackwell, 1996–8.
6 Noha Mellor, *The Making of Arab News*, Lanham MD: Rowman and Littlefield, 2005.
7 Lina Khatib, 'Television and Public Action in the Beirut Spring', in Naomi Sakr (ed.), *Arab Media and Political Renewal: Community, Legitimacy and Public Life*, London: I.B. Tauris, 2007, pp. 28–43.
8 Hugh Mackay, Wendy Maples and Paul Reynolds, *Investigating the Information Society*, London: Routledge, 2001.
9 At a conference in Durham in September 2007, Lina Khatib talked of Internet *fossils*, websites that once had an immediate relevance and were much accessed but that have fallen into past relevance and contemporary non-use. This seems a particularly insightful way to understand the temporary nature of much web-based activity and the communities that produce it.
10 Marc Lynch, *Voices of the New Arab Public: Iraq, al-Jazeera, and Middle East Politics Today*, New York: Columbia University Press, 2006. Also Marc Lynch, *State Interests and Public Spheres: The International Politics of Jordan's Identity*, New York: Columbia University Press, 1999.
11 Marc Lynch, *Voices of the New Arab Public*, p. 3.
12 See, for example, the chapters by Marwan Kraidy, 'Star Academy in Lebanon and Kuwait', Albrecht Hofheinz, 'Arab Internet Use: Popular Trends and Public Impact' and Giovanna Maiola and David Ward, 'Democracy and the Media in Palestine' in Naomi Sakr (ed.), *Arab Media and Political Renewal*, pp. 44–55, 56–79 and 96–117.
13 Jodi Dean, Jon Anderson and Geert Lovink (eds), 'Introduction', in *Reformatting Politics: Information Technology and Global Civil Society*, London: Routledge, 2006.
14 Mamoun Fandy, *(Un)Civil War of Words: Media and Politics in the Arab World*, Oxford: Praeger Security Press, 2007.
15 See also Mamoun Fandy, 'Information Technology, Trust and Social Change in the Arab World', *The Middle East Journal* 54 (3), 2000, pp. 379–98.
16 Naomi Sakr, *Satellite Realms: Transnational Television, Globalization and the Middle East*, London and New York: I.B. Tauris, 2001.
17 *International Herald Tribune*, 'Silencing Arab Media', from http://www.iht.com/bion/printfriendly.php?id=10576531; accessed 29 February 2008.

18 Emma C. Murphy, 'Agency and Space: The Political Impact of Information Technologies in the Arab World', *Third World Quarterly* 27 (6) (2006), pp. 1059–84.
19 United Nations, *Global e-Government Readiness Report 2004*, New York: United Nations, 2004.
20 Noha Mellor, *The Making of Arab News*, p. 5.
21 Guy Debord, *The Society of the Spectacle*, New York: Zone Books, 1994.
22 Barney Warf and John Grimes, 'Counterhegemonic Discourses and the Internet', *The Geographical Review* 87 (2), 1997, p. 267.
23 Ibid., p. 261.
24 Henri Lefebvre, *Critique of Everyday Life*, first published in French in 3 vols, Paris: L'Arche 1947–81.
25 Stephen D. McDowell, Philip E. Steinberg and Tami K. Tomasello, *Managing the Infosphere: Governance, Technology and Cultural Practice in Motion*, Philadelphia: Temple University Press, 2008, pp. 168–9.
26 UNDP/Arab Fund for Economic and Social Development, *Arab Human Development Report 2003: Building a Knowledge Society*, New York: UNDP, 2003.

8

The Impact of Arab Satellite Channels on Public Opinion

―――

Fares Braizat and David Berger

Introduction

What is the impact of Arab satellite television on attitudes and values in the Arab world? Do satellite television stations in the Arab World form, shape, influence and change public opinion, or do they respond to deeply seeded attitudes and values? In other words, do the editorial lines of satellite television stations like al-Jazeera and al-Arabiya reflect opinions held by previously constrained Arab publics or do editorial lines form, shape and change public opinion? These questions have attracted a wide range of academics, writers, journalists, pollsters and policy-makers who have tried to explain and understand the impact of new media on politics and vice versa.

Previous research on the proliferation of satellite television in the Middle East has focused on two areas: quantitative research has explored the degree to which 24-hour news channels magnify anti-American attitudes (Gentzkow and Shapiro, 2003; Nisbet, Scheufele and Shanahan, 2004), and qualitative content analysis has explored the formation of new 'public spheres' in the Arab world (Seib, 2008; Lynch, 2005; Ghareeb, 2000; Anderson and Eickelman, 1999). Quantitative studies found that though anti-American sentiment is widespread in the Arab and Muslim world, satellite television channels appear to magnify this phenomenon. More rigorous quantitative studies found that anti-Americanism is deeply rooted in politics and is not a culture-based phenomenon (Hamarneh, 2005; Braizat, 2006). Discussions of new public spheres have shown that political debate, previously the domain of elites, is now accessible to a wider audience through live televized discussion shows, as well as the advent of call-in shows, blogging and informal online polls.

This study will examine the relationship between satellite television and public opinion in Jordan. Satellite television ownership and Internet access increased significantly in Jordan between 2003 and 2008. Though some theorized that the Internet would become the new media vanguard in the Arab world (Anderson and Eickelman, 1999), our data indicates that television is still considered the primary source for local, regional and international news in Jordan. Despite the widespread notion that elites are more inclined to use the Internet, the data confirms that their media consumption habits are similar to patterns observed among the general public: television is by far the most relied-upon source of information. By using a series of cross-tabulations, this study shows that public opinion differs significantly according to the specific channel that respondents consider to be their 'most trusted source' for local, regional and international news. We focus on viewers of al-Jazeera, al-Arabiya and Jordanian Television, which are the three most popular stations in Jordan as trusted sources of news. We contend that variation in opinions held by viewers across these stations have little to do with the effect of the distinct messages of the stations themselves, but rather result from a selection bias by viewers, who choose stations that have editorial perspectives closely aligned with their own.

TABLE 8.1
Sample sizes for surveys used in this chapter

Survey year	Sample size
2003	1,403
2004	1,386
2005	1,385
2006	1,115
2007	1,132
2008	1,152

The data in this study is drawn from surveys conducted between 2003 and 2008 by the Center for Strategic Studies at the University of Jordan. The Center undertakes yearly surveys to measure the political and social attitudes of Jordanians, as well as their media consumption habits. The sample size is well over 1,000 in each of the surveys and the Center uses a multi-stage cluster technique to ensure that the sample is nationally representative.

Background: the stations and editorial agendas

The explosion of satellite TV ownership and Internet access in the Middle East has changed participation in political dialogues. It is no longer an elite activity focused on few officially mandated topics, but is rather an act that crosses demographic lines and includes a variety of controversial issues important to Arab publics (Anderson and Eickelman, 1999). In order to understand the impact of this phenomenon, it is important to outline the history and editorial agendas of the most prominent stations in Jordan.

Al-Jazeera

Al-Jazeera is based in Doha, Qatar, and began broadcasting in November 1996. It is estimated to reach some 40 million viewers throughout the world.[1] The Emir of Qatar, Sheikh Hamad bin Khalifa al Thani, established the channel and hired an editorial team of some 20 BBC Arabic veterans after their failed attempt to start an objective BBC service in Saudi Arabia. The government of Qatar granted the channel $140 million to finance its first five years of broadcasts, with the understanding that it would become self-sustaining after that point.

The channel's popularity spread rapidly, and in its early days it was hailed by many in the West as a harbinger of a new, more liberal-minded Middle East. During this time, the channel's Jordanian, Kuwaiti and Egyptian bureaus were all briefly shuttered for various perceived insults to the ruling cliques. The station fiercely maintains its independence from Arab governments and delivers an editorial line that is often hostile to these governments, as well as to US involvement in the region and Israel's actions in the continuing conflict with the Palestinians.

After the attacks of 11 September 2001, officials in the United States became highly critical of the station and accused it of acting as a mouthpiece for al-Qaeda. In 2006, al-Jazeera began an English-language service and its Arabic service continues to be the most prominent news source in the Arab world.

The most recent punch levelled by al-Jazeera against moderate governments in the region came during the Israeli attack on Gaza, which took place during December 2008 and January 2009. Al-Jazeera reflected popular opinion by portraying moderate Arab governments as politically bankrupt. Furthermore, it depicted the policies of Israel, the United States and the European Union, as well as European governments individually, as immoral. The attitude of the channel was reflected in the fact that it referred to victims of the Israeli assault on Gaza as 'martyrs', while al-Arabiya referred to them as 'killed'.

Al-Arabiya
A Saudi prince, Sheikh Walid al-Ibrahim, founded al-Arabiya in 2003 specifically to act as a counter-balance to al-Jazeera. The channel broadcasts from Dubai and maintains an editorial policy consistent with the official positions of moderate Arab governments such as Saudi Arabia, Egypt and Jordan. It is also referred to by some media analysts as a collective presentation of official Arab television stations. The editorial policy of al-Arabiya was criticized during the aforementioned Israel assault on Gaza because it did not use the adjective 'martyrs' to describe Palestinian victims.

Jordanian National Television
Jordanian National Television (JTV) was established in 1968 in the aftermath of the 1967 war and Jordan's loss of the West Bank to Israel. At that time, the Jordanian government desperately needed to rally favourable public opinion, especially in the face of an aggressive media campaign by Egypt against the regime. Currently, JTV continues to present the official view of the state and helps to mobilize support for government policies. Political opposition groups did not have a large presence on JTV until after the democratic reforms, which began in 1989. Since then, political opposition groups have occasionally appeared on specific JTV programmes; however, their organizational news is not covered beyond their limited participation in parliament. JTV coverage of anti-government protests was rare until the recent Israeli attack on Gaza. During this crisis, JTV covered demonstrations across the country, showing Jordanian solidarity with the Palestinians in Gaza.

Changing the technological landscape: penetration of satellite and Internet access

Between 2003 and 2008, satellite-dish ownership and Internet access greatly increased in Jordan. As a result, Jordanians are now free to choose from a diverse array of sources from which to obtain their political, social and economic information. Figure 8.1 shows that satellite-dish ownership has increased more rapidly and to a greater degree than Internet access. Availability of operational satellite devices in Jordanian households enables people to access over 300 channels broadcasting in Arabic. A significant number of them are dedicated to news coverage, and they represent a variety of ideologies and political points of view, ranging from al-Qaeda-like discourse to the US government-sponsored al-Hurra TV.

FIGURE 8.1
Percentage of households owning a satellite device

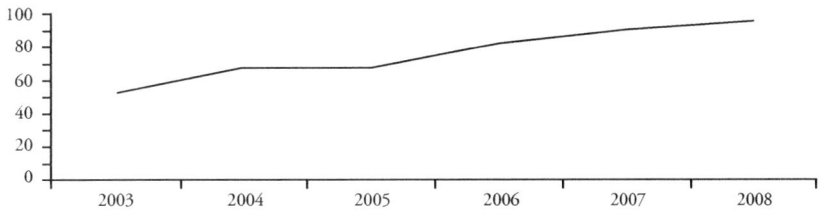

TABLE 8.2
Most trusted sources for 'local news'

Source	2003	2004	2005	2006	2007	2008
TV	73	76	77	78	78	80
Radio	4	4	6	4	4	4
Papers	11	13	11	9	9	10
Magazines	0	0	0	0	0	0
Internet	0	0	0	2	4	2
Friends	5	3	2	4	3	2
Other	2	1	1	1	0	0
DK/NA	4	3	1	2	1	2
Refusal	1	1	2	1	0	0
Total	100	100	100	100	100	100

Given the wide availability of satellite television as well as Internet and newspapers, Jordanians express a clear preference for television as their most trusted medium for news. Tables 8.2, 8.3 and 8.4 show that for local, Arab and international news the vast majority of Jordanians prefer television. For local news, a large majority of Jordanians prefer television broadcasts, though a noticeable minority report newspapers as their most trusted source. The popularity of TV as the most trusted source for local news has increased from 73 per cent in 2003 to 80 per cent in November 2008. Newspapers came second as the most trusted source for local news, and the number of people relying on them has remained almost constant between 2003 and 2008, as shown in Table 8.2.

TABLE 8.3
Most trusted sources for 'Arab regional news'

Source	2003	2004	2005	2006	2007	2008
TV	81	86	84	87	88	88
Radio	4	3	4	2	2	2
Papers	6	5	6	4	4	4
Magazines	0	0	0	0	3	0
Internet	1	0	0	1	1	1
Friends	2	2	1	2	0	2
Other	1	1	1	1	2	0
DK/NA	4	2	1	1	0	3
Refusal	1	1	3	1	0	0
Total	100	100	100	100	100	100

TABLE 8.4
Most trusted sources for 'international news'

Source	2003	2004	2005	2006	2007	2008
TV	80	87	84	88	88	90
Radio	4	2	5	2	2	2
Papers	6	4	5	4	3	2
Magazines	0	0	0	0	0	0
Internet	1	1	1	2	3	2
Friends	2	1	1	2	1	1
Other	1	2	1	1	1	0
DK/NA	5	2	3	1	1	3
Refusal	1	1	0	1	1	0
Total	100	100	100	100	100	100

As of 2008, these findings hold true across demographic categories, with minor variation. Individuals with higher monthly income and monthly expenditures are somewhat more likely to choose newspapers for local news. A similar pattern is present in terms of level of educational attainment. A larger minority of those with secondary or greater than secondary levels of educational attainment receives their local news from newspapers. In terms of age, individuals between the ages of 18 and 34 are more likely than others to list newspapers as their most trusted source of local news, though this proportion is still a minority. Despite these small fluctuations, the vast majority of Jordanians in all demographic categories choose television as their most trusted source of local, regional and international news.

The trend in Jordan shows that television is increasing in prominence as the most trusted source for Arab and international news. In 2003, 80 per cent of respondents reported that TV was their most trusted source for such news. By November 2008, this percentage increased to 88 per cent for Arab news and 90 per cent for international news.

Evidence suggests that the Jordanian public is heavily dependent on visual media for its news, whether local, regional or international. Evaluating the extent to which the media in general and TV in particular makes an impact on or reflects public opinion requires a closer look at the profile of viewers of various channels. Since TV is the most prominent source of news in our sample, it is the news source that we will examine in greater detail in order to shed light on the questions addressed by this chapter.

FIGURE 8.2

Computer and Internet penetration in Jordan: the percentage of adult Jordanians (18+) who use computers and the Internet

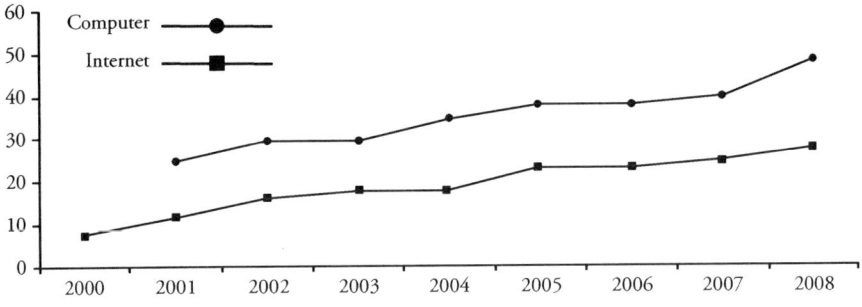

Source: CSS surveys.

The New Arab Media

Satellite television and public opinion

We established that TV is the most trusted source of news for the Jordanian public by asking a direct question to respondents about their preferred news source and giving them a list of media sources to choose from. This question allowed respondents to specify 'other sources' that were not listed, and was followed by another asking respondents to specify the name of the TV station, newspaper, radio, magazine or website they trust most for local, Arab and international news. For example, if a respondent chose TV as the most trusted source of news, he or she was asked to name the particular station he or she trusts most. According to our results, the most popular television stations in Jordan are al-Jazeera, al-Arabiya and Jordanian Television. Jordanian Television has maintained a loyal audience for local news of approximately half of the population since 2003, as shown in Figure 8.3. Al-Jazeera was the most trusted source of local news for nearly a quarter of the population, whereas al-Arabiya did not manage to attract more than 6 per cent. The latter does not provide an alternative source to Jordanian Television because it is not expected to be controversial or to report any local news that JTV would not report. Thus, its influence and appeal as a substitute remains limited. Unlike al-Arabiya, al-Jazeera has developed a reputation for reporting controversial news that will not usually be reported by JTV or al-Arabiya and therefore it attracts curious and critical viewers.

FIGURE 8.3
Sources of local news for Jordanians

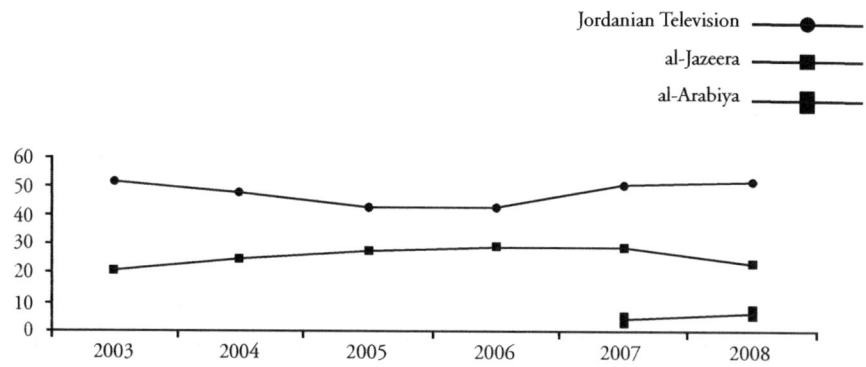

For Arab and international news, a majority of Jordanians chose al-Jazeera (54 per cent Arab and 58 per cent international) followed by al-Arabiya (16 per cent and 17 per cent respectively) and finally Jordanian Television (16 per cent and 14 per cent) as their most trusted news source. These three stations account for 86 per cent of Arab news consumers and 89 per cent of international news consumers. Al-Jazeera's dominance in these domains is unchallenged. Al-Jazeera's share as most trusted source of Arab news has increased from 36 per cent in 2003 to 54 per cent in November 2008. This increase was paralleled by a decline of JTV's share from 32 per cent in 2003 to 16 per cent in November 2008. Although al-Arabiya has doubled its share (8 per cent in 2003 to 16 per cent in 2008) it is not gaining substantially compared to the gains al-Jazeera has managed to acquire over the same period.

FIGURE 8.4
Sources of Arab news for Jordanians

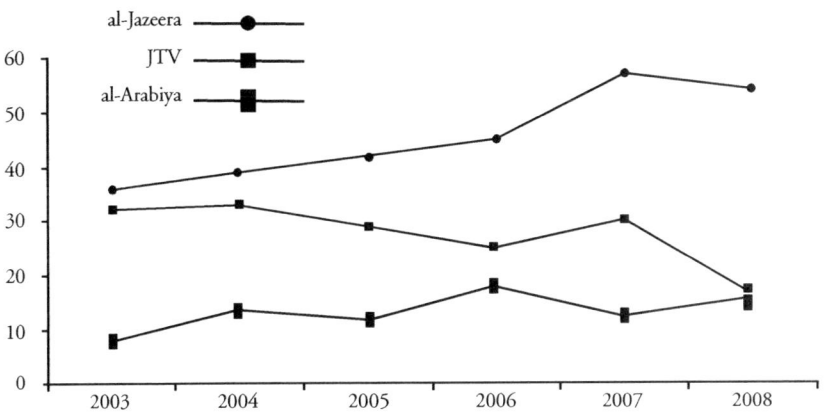

For international news al-Jazeera has grown from 35 per cent in 2003 to a record 58 per cent in 2008. This gain has occurred at the expense of al-Arabiya, which in Jordan has seen a downward trend in its international news viewer figures from 31 per cent in 2003 to a record low of 14 per cent in 2008. JTV also gained viewers from al-Arabiya during this period by increasing its share from 9 per cent in 2003 to 17 per cent in 2008. Al-Arabiya began broadcasting in 2003, shortly before the invasion of Iraq. Initially, it was running neck and neck with al-Jazeera. However, by 2008 it had lost nearly half of its international news audience. The editorial line of al-Arabiya is seen as moderate and pro-USA, and barely critical of Arab governments, particularly in those countries that are close to or allies of Saudi policy.

FIGURE 8.5
Sources of international news for Jordanians

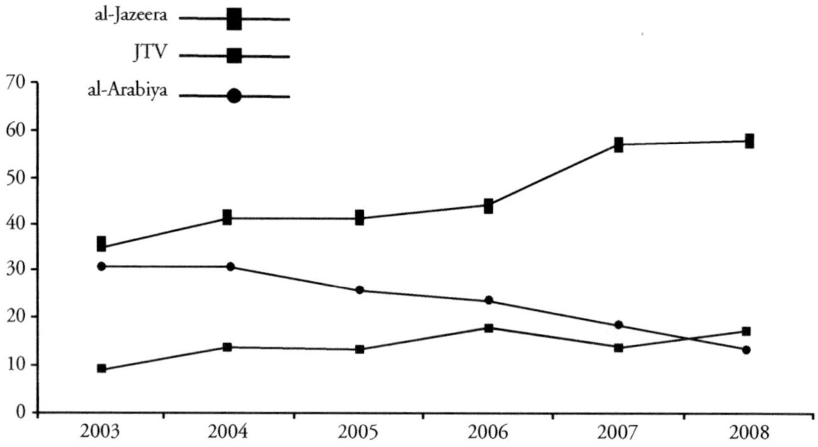

Do viewers differ according to the channel they watch?

After conducting a number of cross-tabulations, we found that the opinions of Jordanians differ significantly across media selection. Within selected channels there are differences between individuals who choose them as their most trusted source for local, regional and international news. In certain cases, al-Jazeera and al-Arabiya viewers largely mirror each other, while in others al-Arabiya and local Jordanian Television viewers hold very similar views.

The 2008 survey asked respondents to identify the system of government that they believe would best solve the problem of poverty in Jordan,[2] a pressing issue for many Jordanians. When this question was disaggregated in terms of the most trusted source of local news, we found that a plurality of viewers of Jordanian Television (42 per cent) and al-Arabiya viewers (41 per cent) and a lower percentage (35 per cent) of al-Jazeera viewers specified a multi-party parliamentary system, whereas the plurality of al-Jazeera viewers (37 per cent) preferred a sharia-based system without elections or political parties, compared to 29 per cent for both al-Arabiya and JTV viewers. The differences are not staggeringly obvious but nonetheless point to a trend that is uncovered in these and other variables; namely, that local al-Jazeera viewers are more likely to favour a religiously informed political system to solve the problem of poverty in Jordan than the viewers of JTV and al-Arabiya.

However, when the same question is cross-tabulated for international news viewers, we find that al-Jazeera viewers are more likely than those of JTV and al-Arabiya to view a multi-party system as the best one to solve the problem of poverty in Jordan. For example, the plurality of Jordanian Television and al-Jazeera viewers favoured a parliamentary multi-party system (34 per cent and 42 per cent, respectively), while a plurality of al-Arabiya viewers (34 per cent) were in favour of a sharia-based government without elections or parties. Al-Arabiya viewers were equally split between a multi-party and sharia-based system (33 per cent and 34 per cent). Only 24 per cent of Jordanian TV viewers and 33 per cent of al-Jazeera viewers supported the sharia-based system.

There is also an interesting reversal between local and international news audiences in terms of electoral participation. The 2008 survey asked Jordanians if they participated in the most recent parliamentary elections, which took place on 20 November 2007.[3] When the results were examined with respect to local news viewer figures, the majority of viewers of the three stations confirmed that they did vote in the elections, with Jordanian Television having the highest majority (63 per cent) followed by al-Jazeera (57 per cent) and al-Arabiya viewers (55 per cent). However, the responses flip when the international news audience is examined. Al-Jazeera and al-Arabiya viewers have the highest proportions of participation (60 per cent each) and Jordanian Television viewers have the lowest (54 per cent). It is clear that the audience for these stations differs not only between each station, but also, importantly, between itself in terms of preferred content.

The trend that al-Jazeera viewers of local news are more likely to have Islamically informed positions has been corroborated by the relationship between voting behaviour and channel viewer figures. In order to gauge the ideological preference, the survey asked respondents to identify which political group they voted for in the last parliamentary election.[4] The majority of viewers of all three stations for local and international news said that they voted for tribal candidates. However, among local news consumers 20 per cent of al-Jazeera viewers said that they supported either the Islamic Action Front, the political party of the Muslim Brotherhood, or non-IAF Islamists, compared to 9 per cent of Jordanian Television viewers and 8 per cent of al-Arabiya viewers. This finding confirms the trend we have uncovered previously with other variables.

The survey asked respondents to choose what they believe to be the most important aspect of democracy. The possible responses were either political (the opportunity to change the government through elections, or the freedom to criticize the government) or socio-economic (closing the gap between rich and poor, or providing basic necessities such as food, housing and clothing to all citizens). Viewers of the three stations agreed that the opportunity to change governments is the most important aspect of democracy. Yet, despite this, significant minorities among them focused on differing aspects of democracy. In terms of local and international news, a higher proportion of viewers of Jordanian Television than of al-Jazeera or al-Arabiya chose 'providing basic necessities', and a large minority of al-Jazeera viewers chose 'closing the gap between rich and poor' as the most important aspect.

Looking internationally, respondents were asked to select what they believe Barack Obama must do to restore America's image in the Middle East.[5] The plurality of international al-Jazeera and Jordanian Television viewers felt that he must solve the Israeli–Palestinian issue, whereas the plurality of al-Arabiya viewers called for ending the occupation of Iraq. Similar proportions hold for regional news consumers. However, for local news viewers, the plurality of al-Arabiya viewers are evenly divided between the Israeli–Palestinian issue and ending the occupation of Iraq.

A greater proportion of viewers of al-Jazeera for international news reported following the last American elections than viewers of the other two stations. This pattern follows for local news viewers as well, though for Arab news viewers, an equal proportion of al-Jazeera and al-Arabiya viewers reported following the elections.

What is the most trusted source of news for the elites?

Although elites in Jordan are state-dependent to a large extent in terms of jobs, contracts and opportunities, they did not turn to the official news channel as their main source of news to follow American elections. Al-Jazeera dominated the news coverage selected by Jordanian elites in respect of the recent presidential elections in the United States. Among our sample of Jordanian elites, political party leaders relied the most on al-Jazeera (70 per cent), followed by statesmen (55 per cent), and the same percentage for journalists, writers and artists. A little over half of professionals (lawyers, medical doctors, pharmacists, engineers, nurses, dentists, geologists and agricultural engineers) relied on al-Jazeera to follow American elections. Among union leaders and university professors only 47 per cent and 45 per cent, respectively, cited al-Jazeera as their main source of news for the American elections. Interestingly, only a third of business elites reported that they relied on al-Jazeera news, as shown in Figure 8.6.

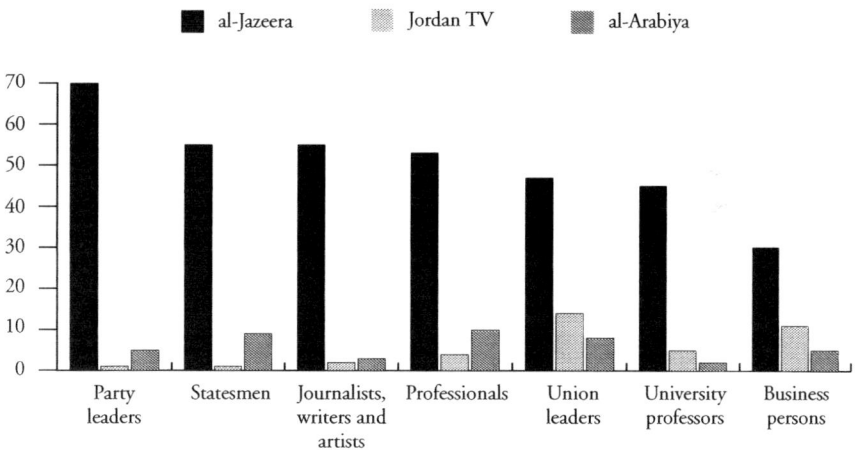

FIGURE 8.6
Sources of news for Jordanian elites regarding American presidential elections of 2008

Source: Center for Strategic Studies, University of Jordan, November 2008.

Whether among the general public or elite, al-Jazeera still dominates the international and regional news scene. This trend points to a significant discrepancy between different types of editorial lines, political leanings, professional coverage and public perceptions of the 'state media'. The fact that the general public as well as elites watch al-Jazeera at the expense of al-Arabiya and JTV speaks to the popularity of the editorial policy of al-Jazeera as opposed to that of al-Arabiya and Jordanian Television. One might argue that al-Jazeera has an advantage because of its funding, number of correspondents and staff in the field. By the same measures, al-Arabiya is comparatively funded, as is the American-sponsored al-Hurra. While al-Arabiya is of marginal importance compared to al-Jazeera, al-Hurra did not even rank as a trusted source of news or as a source to follow American presidential elections. Thus, editorial policy trumps resources in terms of station choice in this matter.

Conclusions

This chapter has outlined ideological profiles of Jordanians in terms of their television consumption habits. We believe that the variation across television station preference, and within television stations, is evidence of selection bias by the audience rather than of the influence of each station's different perspective.

Cognitive studies show that individuals tend to select information sources that conform to their already deeply held beliefs. Furthermore, this is significant in light of research on perception of media bias (Vallone, Ross and Lepper, 1985). Individuals with pre-existing loyalties are likely to concentrate on hostile aspects of media coverage and perceive that the coverage will sway non-partisans in an opposing direction. Al-Jazeera's programming largely conforms to its slogan '*Ar-rai wa ar-rai akher*' or 'The point of view, and the other point of view'. Its talk shows regularly feature Islamists, secularists, American and Israeli guests, as well as a variety of Arab academics, writers and officials. This pot-luck of information and ideas is fertile ground for 'bias assimilation', a phenomenon in which, given ambiguous information, individuals accept at face value information that supports their position but that is highly critical of opposing information. This phenomenon is useful in understanding the difference between viewers of al-Jazeera for local news and for regional and international news. Jordanian Television and newspapers dominate local news consumption in Jordan. Though some papers in Jordan have a degree of editorial freedom, they all tend to closely adhere to the official line followed by the national television station. Given that individuals tend to avoid information sources adverse to previously held beliefs, it is likely that the small number of respondents who expressed a preference for al-Jazeera for local news is disproportionately made up of oppositionists. In Jordan, the Islamic Action Front, which is the political face of the Muslim Brotherhood, is the most active and organized opposition group. Thus, those who choose al-Jazeera for local news are likely representative of this organization, and thus more likely to be in favour of a religious government and less likely to participate in elections that they perceive as rigged in favour of loyalist candidates. The selection bias argument is bolstered by the finding that only 6 per cent of local news viewers choose al-Arabiya, a station that stands close to government lines. Thus, local news consumers either desire the official Jordanian editorial line or the more Islamist aspects of al-Jazeera's programming.

Gentzkow and Shapiro, using regression modelling, found that viewers of satellite television in the Arab world are somewhat more anti-American in their views than other media consumers. Though Gentzkow and Shapiro's model controlled for a number of economic and social variables, it is impossible to accurately control for individuals choosing to congregate in similar ideological communities. Information from Jordan may indicate that individuals tend to pick news sources that are aligned with pre-existing ideas. However, any interaction effect that may occur between viewers and satellite channels is not measured. Thus, disaggregating public opinion along television station choice may provide a clearer breakdown of ideological positions by measuring individuals in terms of the discourse groups into which they self-select.

The profound growth of technological penetration into the Middle East, combined with a blossoming of new Arab-language media, allows media consumers in the region more choices than ever before. However, more choice can mean greater freedom to choose ideological affinity groups rather than exposure to different ideas.

Notes

1 New York Times "Times Topics: Al Jazeera" http://topics.nytimes.com/top/reference/timestopics/organizations/a/al_jazeera/index.html?scp=4&sq=Al%20Jazeera&st=cse, 14 January 2009, retrieved on 21 January 2009.
2 Q405: In your opinion, from these systems what is the best political system to solve the problem of poverty in Jordan?, 2008 Survey, Center for Strategic Studies.
3 Q901: Did you vote in the last parliamentary elections (20/11/2007)? 2008 Survey, Center for Strategic Studies.
4 Q902, To which of the following political groups/trends you voted in the last parliamentary elections?
5 V305.

9

Jordan's Local Radio Revolution: Progress, Challenges and Possibilities

Mahjoob Zweiri

There are currently 19 privately registered radio stations in Jordan, none of which existed prior to 2002. As part of the wider governmental drive to liberalize media markets the audiovisual sector was opened up to investment in 2002 and in that year the Audiovisual Commission was set up to develop and regulate the sector. The first community radio station was introduced in 2006, sponsored by UNESCO.[1] This study will assess the role and impact of this rapidly emerging media sector. In particular it will consider the potential of radio to play a role in increasing participation and political engagement, a core component of the United Nations' Millennium Development Goals (MDGs).

At this early stage in the life of private radio in Jordan it is first necessary to assess its direction of travel. An appraisal of the successes of private radio stations, and perhaps more importantly the challenges faced by them, will be used to suggest a possible future for this Arab 'radio revolution'. The study is based on a series of in-depth interviews with authorized representatives of nine of Jordan's private radio stations. The interviews served to shed light on how the stations perceive themselves in terms of their aims, role, funding and use of technology. As well as the in-depth interviews, the study draws upon publicly available information, including the 2007 media survey carried out by Harris Interactive, which included 2,912 face-to-face interviews on a representative sample throughout Jordan to map present media habits, including a detailed section on the radio. (Details of our interview schedule are in the appendix.)

The study intends to open the door to further debate concerning the role of radio in Jordan and in the broader Middle East.

Background

In recent years there has been a growing recognition and consensus that information and communication technologies (ICTs) are crucial to meeting global development targets. Indeed, the present lack of success in meeting the MDGs identified at the 2005 Millennium Summit in New York can in part be attributed to a failure to tap into the potential contribution of ICTs. ICTs have huge potential power in terms of reaching people, encouraging them to participate in political and social concerns, increasing interactive communication in the delivery of education and health services and opening up economic opportunities in a variety of ways.[2]

This understanding of their significance is enshrined in MDG target 18, which aspires to, 'in cooperation with the private sector make available the benefits of new technologies, especially information and communications'.[3] Efforts to meet this objective have had mixed results in the Arab region. As a recent report by the United Nations and the League of Arab States points out, Arab countries still lag far behind international averages in terms of fixed telephone lines, personal computers and Internet users.[4] Furthermore, there are marked disparities between Arab countries, with populations in the Gulf Cooperation Council (GCC) countries having far greater access than those in other Arab countries. It should, however, be noted that the MDGs are focused entirely on a particular definition of ICTs. The measures of success used include number of telephone lines, cellular subscribers, personal computers in use and Internet users per 100 population. Radio is a notable omission from these means of measurement. Sameer Padania and Francesca Silvani have referred to a 'radio revolution' and pointed out that radio has an important role to play due to its extremely wide penetration and reach.[5] Radio has the potential to have a profound impact on both the MDGs and wider priorities in the Arab region. Radio should not be excluded from discussions of the importance of ICTs: indeed, as shall be considered below, there is potential for radio to have a mutually positive and sustaining role with other ICTs.

The joint UN and League of Arab States (LAS) report referred to above, which considered progress towards the MDGs in the Arab region, focused its attention on youth, noting that these are the 'core stakeholders, beneficiaries of, and instruments for the achievement of the MDGs'.[6] The report noted a 'window of opportunity' due to the anticipated high numbers of working-age population relative to dependants over the next few decades. In order for the benefits of this window of opportunity to be realized, youths must be successfully engaged in active social and political participation. There are also potential risks associated with this young population if its energies are not channelled, including emigration and political frustration leading to violence and extremism.[7] The report noted four pressing issues facing youth development in the Arab region; regional political instability, violence and conflict; education and employment; political and social participation; and health and environment. Most visibly, perhaps, the role of the media and ICTs may be greatest in the realms of political and social participation, since they provide obvious opportunities to inform and engage. There is, however, a slippage between these categories: a more informed and engaged public will have a knock-on effect on each of the other issues, just as they can better equip populations for that engagement. This is particularly crucial when it comes to the region's youth: 'The marginalization of youth poses a threat to good governance of development, since most of the region's development challenges (poverty, unemployment, health problems, etc.) require the engagement of youth if they are to be effectively met.'[8]

It is within this context that this study will consider the evolving media environment in Jordan. In particular, we will consider the potential of radio to play a decisive role in exploiting this 'window of opportunity' for meeting developmental goals as well as broader socio-political objectives in the region. In this sense Jordan provides a test case, being as it is a part of a wider surge in FM radio use in Arab countries.[9] The recent past in Jordan has seen rapid movement in the spread and impact of private radio and, more particularly, community radio – a phenomenon that deserves the attention of policy-makers and academics alike.

Radio and ICTs in Jordan

Changes in the radio sector are only a small part of the current drive in Jordan to open up the ICT sector to investment, a process that is understood to be a means to economic and human development, specifically for reducing unemployment.[10] However, radio is somewhat lost in this process, as the focus of attention has been the more advanced technologies such as the Internet and mobile phones. For example, the 2005 United Nations Economic Social Commission for Western Asia

(ESCWA) *National Profile for the Information Society in Jordan* contains no mention of radio. In the 2007 version of the report there is a tacit acknowledgement of this omission in the aside that '[w]hen they're not at work, Jordanians spend most of their time watching TV or listening to the radio'. However, the role and impact of the radio is still not fully explored in the report, which instead is overwhelmingly focused on computer and telephone technologies,[11] offering a limited vision of what the information society may mean for Jordan. It is therefore unsurprising that the report concludes that 'the role of the media in the information society is currently limited to providing news, social and cultural information and there is very little interest in developing an information society. In other words, the media offers very little benefit in this field.'[12] In a sense, as the analysis that follows will outline, the ESCWA analysis is quite correct: ICTs understood in terms of technological advancement are crucial to contemporary development strategy. However, it should also be noted that there are ways in which radio has demonstrated that it can make a positive contribution to the information society, notably in terms of the need noted above for greater engagement and participation of citizens. Radio deserves greater attention because it provides a low-cost and convenient means to access information. It may not be the main source of information for many people: well-educated, tech-savvy young people in particular will now turn primarily to the Internet or mobile phone technology and the massive communicative potential that these hold. It is right, therefore, that these are at the centre of policy thinking, and satisfying that there have been clear successes in their proliferation.[13] But while the aim of development policy should be to get society as a whole to this stage, it must show full awareness that it is not yet there.[14] There remain significant sections of society that do not possess the technological skills or financial resources needed to access the more advanced technologies. For them, radio plays a substantial role in their efforts to be informed members of society. Moreover, there is a growing tendency for technologies to overlap and reinforce one another in their message distribution efforts, and it should be considered how radio listening might form a symbiotic relationship with use of other ICTs. As we will see, *how* radio manifests itself is crucial to its contribution towards, or impact on, an information society.

Initiating private radio in Jordan: the case of Amman Net

The radio station Amman Net was originally broadcast only through the Internet. In 2000, private radio ownership and broadcasting was still illegal in Jordan. Amman Net founder Daoud Kuttab noted, however, that the Internet, which was not censored, could serve as a platform for radio broadcasts, consequently establishing his radio station via the Internet. Amman Net, therefore, from its inception, provides a good example of the intersection of Internet and radio technologies. The station was then broadcast back on FM frequencies from Palestine, in effect becoming the first private radio station in Amman.

As the name indicates, Amman Net focuses its coverage on local issues in the Jordanian capital. Kuttab asserts that 'enough media is escaping local issues by covering regional and international news, but we didn't want to do that'.[15] His comments echo an established criticism of the Arab media, made for example by Mamoun Fandy, that high-profile television stations such as al-Jazeera and al-Arabiya avoid creating any dissent at home by focusing their attention only on regional or international news, rather than (often negative) local news that might be of importance.[16] Kuttab raises an important point about the role of radio in promoting engagement with local issues. Indeed, Amman Net sees itself as playing a social role in engaging with, and responding to, people who would not otherwise have a voice. If the objective of development policy is to engage people in active social and political participation, this kind of radio offers a powerful tool.

In 2005, following the 2002 legalization of private radio, Amman Net became an FM radio station and it has since been renamed as al-Balad. As its representative told us, it still believes it has a strong social agenda of empowerment, indeed even functioning as a 'non-governmental organization'. Its attention is still focused particularly on 'the marginalized and poor people'. 'Our station is also distinguished by covering so many activities and events that other radio stations don't seek to cover or talk about. We have the ability and the coverage to open hidden issues when other radio stations couldn't do it.'

Part of the reason that al-Balad can make this claim is that it is one of only two radio stations (the other being Sawt al-Madinah) that are legally allowed to broadcast political content, having paid an additional fee.[17] In our interviews, when asked 'What kind of programmes does your radio station present?', the al-Balad representative was the only one to make any reference to political comment. Al-Balad is also the only station to claim that its programmes are designed to represent peoples' interests or problems.

A second possible reason for Amman Net/al-Balad's political focus lies in its having been originally established on the back of Internet technology. When asked how technological advances might have helped the station, the al-Balad representative explained how they made it possible to obtain a lot of information, fast, and also to remove difficulties faced by rules that might otherwise prevent access to information. Internet technology offered a degree of freedom to pursue the original Amman Net vision. The shift to life as a private FM station seems not to have altered this original idea and al-Balad still operates a website containing news and political and social comment. Finally, perhaps the critical key to the ability of al-Balad to continue with this agenda is its source of funding. It stated that the station receives no funding from advertisements. It operates as a non-profit organization and receives funding from various (unspecified) organizations for each programme produced: 'foundations and international organizations support our programs'. As we will see, this funding strategy stands in contrast to the majority of private radio stations operating in Jordan today.

The growth and role of private radio

Of the 18 private radio stations that have emerged in Jordan since 2002, the vast majority focus their attention on offering or reflecting on popular culture and popular music. There is an obvious reason for this: all but two of the stations we spoke to receive 100 per cent of their funding from advertisements. The two exceptions are al-Balad (above), and Melody, which is funded by its sister television station. Therefore, the majority of stations are existentially motivated by advertising revenues; and popular culture and music, it appears, are seen as the most amenable accompaniment to advertising.

There are, however, important exceptions to this rule. Several stations do find air time for social content. Play described its 'social campaigns', 'awareness programs' and 'charity campaigns'. Sawt al-Ghad spoke of its 'youth programmes' and programmes dealing with women's issues, and Rotana of how its 'programmes talk and solve social, emotional and humanitarian issues'. There is therefore a sense in which these advertising-revenue-funded stations are attempting to address social concerns. It is of note, however, that none actually made mention of news information content in the interviews. The pertinent question thus appears to be: how can audience members consider social or political issues in an informed way if they are listening to a radio station that provides little or no contextual social or political information?

The results of the Harris Interactive Jordan Media Survey show that the advertisers have got it right. According to the survey, by far the most popular station of those listening to the radio over a period of seven days was Fann FM, a station dedicated to music, which had a huge 32.2 per cent audience share. The station in second place, Quran FM, bucked the trend, being a station with religious and other content. In total, seven of the top-ten-ranked stations were those offering music or popular culture content; together, they drew a total of 83.3 per cent of audience share. By comparison, and according to the survey, Amman Net had only 0.7 per cent of audience share.

However, the survey also included a striking contradiction: despite the fact that music channels had an 83.3 per cent audience share, when asked what their favourite programme over the past seven days was only 19.7 per cent of respondents replied 'music'. The highest rating, at 26.2 per cent, was for the show of Mohammed al Wakeel, which also includes a lot of music. But even if the above two figures are taken together, the figure of 45.9 per cent for a music-based favourite programme is still markedly disparate from the 83.3 per cent audience share for stations with principally music content. It is worth noting that a popular feature of Wakeel's show is that it offers the opportunity for listeners to voice their local concerns. As one blogger describes:

> These can include complaints about stray dogs, the water being cut off, buses not adhering to their prescribed routes or people in need of help for costly operations or medical care. After hearing people's problems, often after asking what the person has done to remedy the issue, al Wakeel calls the government person in charge and tells him about the problem. The typical conversation with the official starts with the usual pleasantries. After that, Wakeel either tells him the problem or plays the taped call back to the official. The official either knows about the problem and explains its details, asks for time to ask about the problem or asks the person with the problem to visit his office. Sometimes Wakeel bluntly interrogates the official

about specific details, which is the trademark of the show (that is why they call it *bisaraha*; in all frankness).[18]

This description of Wakeel's programme is not so different from the project for local social and political engagement envisioned by Amman Net/al-Balad. However, it differs significantly from the views most often expressed in our interviews with radio station representatives, the majority of whom saw their station's role as one of providing popular music and entertainment content.

A further point of interest arises from the fact that 19 per cent of respondents in the survey stated that programmes devoted to the Qur'an or religious matters were their favourites, while 10.8 per cent said that news programmes were their preferred option, the latter being a surprising statistic given the tiny proportion of shows that are dedicated to news content. It seems that when it comes to radio programming, people are not necessarily getting what they want, or being correctly understood by the majority of private radio stations, despite the apparent popularity of entertainment format shows.

A tension appears to exist, therefore, between the crucial and growing role played by private investment in the media sector, which is justifiably encouraged for the sake of maximizing the impact on the economy, and the potential for radio to encourage political and social participation. That is not to say that private advertisement-based finance leads to the exclusion of social issues. However, it does seem to play a major role in determining the perception of radio station personnel as to their role. Only three stations we spoke to saw part of their role as being to provide news, and only al-Balad also encourages comment and participation on local news items. Al-Watan has lengthy discussion shows that discuss regional news items. At least part of the reason for this is, of course, because only al-Balad and Sawt al-Madinah have a licence to air political content. It is an open question, however, whether other privately financed stations would take up this role if they were permitted to do so.

What the research overwhelmingly demonstrates is that a minority of radio stations are encouraging active participation in social and political issues, but these comprise a popular and important minority nonetheless, and one that could be enlarged with the right encouragement by more visionary radio-station leaders. Initiative is required if the potential of radio to engage people in these issues is to be realized. Evidence shows that the private sector is unlikely to finance this initiative and therefore alternative funding must be forthcoming if such projects are to be a success.

The answer to the broad question of whether radio can contribute to an information society is therefore not entirely bleak simply because this is a lower profile and less sophisticated technology. There already exist positive signs that radio might – in the right conditions – play a substantial role. This argument can be further developed in terms of the integrated use of new technologies, target and actual audiences, and the recent emergence of community radio.

Technology
The capacity of radio to work in tandem with other ICTs is crucial. As we have seen, the pioneer of private radio in Jordan, Amman Net, was from its inception tied to the Internet, and the ability to stream radio through the Internet can be seen as a pivotal factor in the subsequent spread of private radio in Jordan. The fusion of the two technologies has played a part in the rise in numbers of private radio stations. Almost all of the representatives of radio stations that we interviewed spoke about the role of the Internet in increasing their audiences. The representative of Mazaj, for example, commented that 'having a website on the net helped by raising the size of the audience and enables people from all over the world to keep in touch'. Mobile telephony was also remarked upon by several of the stations. The interviewee for Watan, for example, said that 'cell phones allowed people to contact us to participate in the programs, wherever they are'. These illustrations of the intersection of radio, technology and the more advanced technologies commonly associated with the information society suggest that the potential for radio to promote participation in broader technological developments should not be underestimated. Equally, this link has advanced the potential for radio itself, having provided radio stations with far greater, and much speedier, access to information. All of the representatives of radio stations that we interviewed spoke of the power that the Internet has to keep them in touch with people and events around the world.

Technology of course comes at a cost, which presents a twofold dilemma. In terms of radio stations, it brings us back to the fraught question of funding. They are reliant on their sources of revenue to provide them with the money to buy technologies – the more expensive the technology, the more dependent they are on the preferences and requirements of their sponsors. For the listeners, a widely disseminated radio might promote the use of other technologies, but this can only be effective if those technologies are accessible and affordable.

It is reasonable to conclude, therefore, that while the intersection between radio and other ICTs offers one potential route for the expansion and deepening of the information society, that process is not necessarily inevitable but rather depends on broader issues relating to cost and accessibility of the range of ICTs.

Audience
Another positive feature to note about the role of radio is its particular appeal to specific target and actual audiences. If we return to the developmental priorities, a core objective must be to open up the information society to those who are presently not engaged with it. It is therefore of note that in the Harris interviews, of the total number of interviewees that had listened to the radio in the last seven days 26.6 per cent had less than a secondary education. This compares to 25.4 per cent of mobile phone users, 18.4 per cent of those who read a daily newspaper, and 8.4 per cent of total email users. Radio is therefore the media that has the greatest potential for reaching out to the less educated and perhaps poorest represented section of society.

Turning to the 'window of opportunity' already described, the young must also be a particular target in efforts to educate and engage if the benefits of an information society are to be reaped. All but one of the radio station representatives that we spoke to stated that their principal target audience was young people. This is unsurprising given the high proportion of young people in the Jordanian population (approximately 32 per cent are under the age of 14) and it suggests a coincidence of interest between radio stations and government development policy, which is generally succeeding in terms of actual audience make-up. The Harris survey revealed that 72.2 per cent of all radio audiences are under 39 years of age and 54.1 per cent under 30. Radio may thus be said to hold a particular power to reach such a broad and prolific section of young people; one that can usefully be exploited by the champions of both private radio and the information society.

Community-based radio

ICTs are recognized as an important means for encouraging community-based dialogue, for supporting community-based projects and for forming a conduit through which communities can engage with the wider world, all of which are considered crucial components of the drive for economic development.[19] Radio has a particular salience in this regard.

The historical philosophy of community radio is to use this medium as the voice of the voiceless, the mouthpiece of oppressed people (be it on racial, gender or class grounds) and generally as a tool for development.[20]

Community-based radio involves bringing together key stakeholders from the community to actively participate in the creation of a radio station. It is recognized by the United Nations Educational, Scientific and Cultural Organization (UNESCO) as an important component of its media policy, due to community radio's ability to harness the 'inclusive and transformative power of converging technologies'.[21] As a growing number of cases has shown, community-based radio is a very conducive medium through which to achieve developmental objectives. Padania and Silvani's study of community radio in Africa, for instance, documents an excellent example of how successful community-based radio can encourage dialogue, participation and the use of new technologies by members of the community who might not otherwise have access to them.[22] Community-based radio has also begun to play an important part in the story of private radio in Jordan.

The original Internet-streamed Amman Net was in many ways a community-based project when it began in 2000. However, the first true community radio station was established in Jordan in 2006. UNESCO sponsored the establishment of a radio station in Lib and Mleih that ran hand in hand with an e-village project, which was sponsored by UNIFEM.[23] The radio station aims to empower citizens' through participation: the station is managed by the local community, and surveys have been used to determine what kinds of programmes will be scheduled. Amman Net was involved in providing local people with training in the use of media technology.[24] The two projects present outstanding potential to inform and engage the local population, and simultaneously to promote the use of ICTs. The station has been used to 'raise awareness of the community to issues related to the development of the community including education, health, freedom of expression, democracy'.[25] Amman Net was involved in supporting the establishment of the radio station and in our interview the al-Balad representative said that 'we helped in the launch of other radio stations; we are a non-governmental organization that contributes in the training of their cadres, especially in places that need this media to convey their voices'.

A sign of the significance of Jordan's (albeit relatively late) entrance into community radio was that in 2006 it became the first Arab country to host the World Assembly of Community Radio Broadcasters Conference. The conference was organized by the Association Mondiale des Radiodiffuseurs Communautaires (AMARC), an NGO that aims to promote community-based radio globally. The AMARC president, Steve Buckley, commented that Jordan was awarded the role of host because of its 'significant steps in opening the airwaves to include community radio'.[26] The positive moves in the direction of community radio continued with the establishment of two further community-based stations. Yarmouk FM, in Irbid, was set up by the Journalism Department at Yarmouk University. More recently, Farah al Nas FM has begun broadcasting, sponsored by the Queen Zein Al-Sharaf Institute, the Jordanian Fund for Human Resources and Development (JOHUD) and a grant from the United States' State Department and Bureau of Democracy, Human Rights and Labour. The station intends to encourage the participation of young people and will focus on social issues, particularly concerning women and young people. Promisingly, it will offer training to 10-to 24-year-olds to take part in the running of the station and in the use of media technology. JOHUD's deputy executive director, Eman Nimri, commented that: 'By serving as an entry-way through which issues can be brought to light to the general public and decision-makers, Farah al-Nas will encourage suitable solutions to be reached.'[27]

For all these positive indicators of the growing contribution of community radio in Jordan, there has been a recent sign that the velocity of travel has faltered. In December 2007 a licence to set up a community-based radio station in the town of Zarqa was turned down.[28] This leaves open the question of whether community radio will be able to continue to grow and realize its potential contribution to the information society in Jordan.

Conclusion

The surge in the proliferation of Jordanian private radio stations can be seen as part of the broader expansion of media technologies in the Arab region. However, despite the massive expansion in the number of private sector stations, radio is not currently playing a decisive role in Jordan in increasing political engagement and there is at best a mixed picture for its contribution to an information society. Radio stations are overwhelmingly devoted to apolitical issues and rarely engage people with political and social issues that are important to them. They are also hamstrung by a lack of media professionals.

However, a complex picture is emerging in which there are signs of hope. The diversity of stations and audiences presented by radio is key to the role it could potentially play. Our analysis reveals both the profound potential and existing pitfalls of the role of radio in the Jordanian information society. Some stations are attempting to inform people and engage them in political and social issues. However, this is being hampered by the reliance on advertisement funding and government licences. Radio stations are promoting the use of other technologies and therefore contributing to the growing ability of citizens to obtain information and engage interactively with others. But this promotion is again dependent upon the availability of resources for purchasing these technologies, or otherwise making them accessible, and the development of skills (both among media professionals and audiences) that enable them to be used effectively. Radio has an impressive spread and reach, and its audiences are representative of the target groups that are most crucial to the future development of the information society. Local community-based radio, in particular, has proven itself as an empowering media that can help move developmental agendas forward, providing a means for local engagement and opportunities for training local participants in the use of media technology. But, as this chapter has argued, these remain in a fragile state and require financial and political support if they are to continue to develop.

As Padania and Silvani make clear, radio is not a 'silver bullet'.[29] It does, however, present a productive way forward towards a number of political priorities in the Arab region: both developmental and geo-political. It is important because it is a media form that reaches otherwise marginalized sections of society. It offers one way of helping the 'window of opportunity' to be realized. However, in order for this to happen policy must be supportive of the kinds of radio that inform and engage citizens, and donors must be found to fund ambitious new projects, without the constraints dictated by a reliance on advertising revenues or political compliance, most likely NGOs and international organizations. The evolving encounter with radio in Jordan thus raises questions and holds important lessons for the wider Arab region.

Notes

1. See http://portal.unesco.org/ci/en/ev.php-URL_ID=21934&URL_DO=DO_PRINTPAGE&URL_SECTION=201.html. 27 April 2006
2. G. Weigel and D. Waldburger (eds), 'ICT4D – Connecting People for a Better World – Lessons, Innovations and Perspectives of Information and Communication Technologies in Development'; Swiss Agency for Development and Corporation (SDC) and the Global Knowledge Partnership (GKP), 2004.
3. UN Millennium Project, *Investing in Development: A Practical Plan to Achieve the Millennium Development Goals*, New York: Earthscan, 2005, p. xix.
4. The United Nations and The League of Arab States, *The MDGs in the Arab Region 2007: A Youth Lens*, 2007, http://www.uis.unesco.org/template/pdf/EducGeneral/MDGsArab07.pdf; accessed 15 July 2008.
5. Sameer Padania and Francesca Silvani, 'Local Radio in the Information Society: Technology, Participation and Content in Africa', in *Information and Communication Technologies and Large-scale Poverty Reduction Lessons from Asia, Africa, Latin America and the Caribbean*, London: Panos, 2005.
6. The United Nations and The League of Arab States, p. 30.
7. The United Nations and The League of Arab States, p. 28.
8. The United Nations and The League of Arab States, p. 30.
9. See *The Arab World's FM Radio Boom Continues with 36 New FM Radio Stations Starting Between Late 2005 and Jan 2007*, http://www.ameinfo.com/111362.html; accessed 16 July 2007.
10. United Nations Economic Social Commission for Western Asia (ESCWA), *National Profile for the Information Society in Jordan*, ESCWA, 2005.
11. See *Information Society Measurement: Policies and Indicators*, http://css.escwa.org.lb/ICTpolicymaking/14.pdf; accessed 16 July 2008.
12. ESCWA, *National Profile*, p. 13.
13. ESCWA, *National Profile*, p. 14
14. In 2002 Kai Hafez pointed out that

   > [t]hose who believe that political transformation is essentially a 'mass' phenomenon created by social movements must conclude that for the next decades the Internet will probably be less influential than radio, TV, the press, or even underground videos and cassettes.

However, anyone assuming that politics is elitist could also maintain that even the small number of mostly upper- and upper-middle-class users of the Internet might be conducive to political change.

The spread of Internet technology has improved since 2002, but the point largely still holds true. See Kai Hafez, 'Guest Editor's Introduction: Mediated Political Communication in the Middle East', *Political Communication* 19 (2), 2002, pp. 1214.

15 'Interview with Daoud Kuttab', in *Arab Media and Society* (February 2007).
16 Mamoun Fandy, *(Un)Civil War of Words: Media and Politics in the Arab World*, Westport, CT and London: Praeger Security International, 2007.
17 *Two Radio Stations Launch in Jordan*, http://www.mebjournal.com/component/option,com_magazine/func,show_article/id,102/; accessed 16 July 2008.
18 'In all frankness', http://ajloun.blogspot.com/2006/07/in-all-frankness.html; accessed 17 July 2008.
19 For discussions of related issues see Leigh Keeble and Brian D. Loader (eds), *Community Informatics: Shaping Computer-Mediated Social Relations*, London: Routledge, 2001.
20 Lumko Mtimde, Marie-Hélène Bonin, Nkopane Maphiri and Kodjo Nyamaku, *What is Community Radio? A Resource Guide*, AMARC, Africa and PANOS, 1998.
21 UNESCO, 'Medium Term Strategy for 2008–13', UNESCO, 2007, http://portal.unesco.org/ci/en/ev.php-URL_ID=25761&URL_DO=DO_TOPIC&URL_SECTION=201.html; accessed 20 July 2008.
22 Padania and Silvani, 'Local Radio in the Information Society'.
23 'Minister of ICT visits e-village project in the governorate of Madaba', http://www.unifem.org.jo/pages/articledetails.aspx?aid=476; accessed 21 July 2008.
24 UNIFEM Economic Security and ICT Program, *E-Pulse*, April–June 2007, http://www.unifem.org/attachments/products/epulse_02_eng.pdf; accessed 21 July 2008.
25 See http://portal.unesco.org/ci/en/ev.php-URL_ID=21934&URL_DO=DO_TOPIC&URL_SECTION=201.html; accessed 27 April 2006.
26 See http://www.encyclopedia.com/doc/1G1-141042127.html; accessed 19 January 2006.
27 See 'Youth-run Radio Station to Launch in Jordan', http://www.internews.org/prs/2008/20080519_jordan.shtm.
28 www.i4donline.net/news/news-details.asp?NewsID=12943.
29 Padania and Silvani, 'Local Radio in the Information Society', p. 33.

Appendix

Private radio stations

Radio station status	Programme manager	Date of interview	Frequency	Name of the radio station	Company name	Number
			92.00	(Mood FM)	al-Nawares Company	1
			102.5	(Beat FM)	al-Nawares Company	2
ON	Ramzy al-Halaby	14/1/2008	99.6	(Play FM)	Modern Media	3
OFF				(Sawt Amman)	Modern Media	4
ON	Tareq Abu Laghad	14/1/2008	95.3	(Mazaj FM)	Arab Media Network	5
ON	George Shurfan	21/1/2008	101.5	(Sawt el Ghad FM)	Jordan National Radio Broadcasting	6
ON	Sawsan Zaydeh	17/1/2008	92.4	(Amman Net/ Sawt el Moujtamaa/ (al-Balad FM)	David Qitab and Partners	7
ON	Ely Fares	20/1/2008	Amman 99.9 Irbid 90.5	(Rotana FM)	al-Qawn Company for Radio and TV Broadcasting	8
ON	Mahmoud al-Rajaby	17/1/2008	104.7	(Hayat FM)	al-Salam Radio Broadcasting	9
ON	Yosor Hassan	16/1/2008	Amman 100.3 Irbid 100.7	(Watan)	al-Rawae' Company for Radio and TV Broadcasting	10

Radio station status	Programme manager	Date of interview	Frequency	Name of the radio station	Company name	Number
ON	Yaser Fahmy	20/1/2008	88.5	(Sawt al-Madeena FM)	al-Baddad Media and Communications	11
			97.1	(Ahlen FM)	al-Deka Broadcasting	12
			93.7	(Nojoum)	International Company	13
ON	Hamdan al-Faory	27/1/2008	Amman 91.1 Zarqa 105.5	(Melody)	Jordanian Company for Radio and TV	14
OFF				Spin (Arabic)	Modern Company for Radio Broadcasting	15
OFF				Spin (English)	Modern Company for Radio Broadcasting	16
			Lib Mleih	al-Qaria	Community-based: sponsored by UNESCO	17
			105.7 Irbid	Yamouk FM	Community-based	18
	Haitham Atoom		98.5 Amman Zarqa	Farah al-Nas	Community-based: sponsored by Queen Zein al-Sharaf institute, JOHUD and the US state department	19

Government-owned radio stations

Radio station status	Manager name	Date of interview	Frequency	Radio station name	Company name	Number
ON			90.3 Ma'an	(Ma'an FM)	al-Hussein Bin Talal University	1
ON			105.7 Irbid	(Yarmouk FM)	al-Yarmouk University	2
ON			89.5	(Amen FM)	Public Security Directorate	3
ON			102.1 104.2	(Fann FM)	Jordan Armed Forces	4
ON			93.1 Amman 91.5 Aqaba 89.7 Irbid	(al-Quran al-Qareem)	Ministry of Awqaf and Islamic Affairs	5

International radio stations

Radio station status	Manager name	Date of interview	Frequency	Radio station name	Company name	Number
ON			Amman 103.1 Ajloun 89.1	BBC	British Broadcasting Corporation	1
ON			Amman 98.1 Ajloun 107.4	SAWA	Organization of US International Broadcasters	2

Further Reading

Alterman, J. B., *New Media, New Politics? From Satellite Television to the Internet in the Arab World*, Washington Institute for Near East Policy, 1998.

Anderson, J. and Eickelman, D., *New Media in the Muslim World*, Bloomington, IN: Indiana University Press, 2000.

Avraham, E., *Behind Media Marginality: Coverage of Social Groups and Places in the Israeli Press*, Lanham, MD: Lexington Books, 2003.

Boler, M., *Digital Media and Democracy: Tactics in Hard Times*, Cambridge, MA: The MIT Press, 2008.

Bouzid, A., *Framing the Struggle: Essays on the Middle East and the US Media*, New York: Universe Publishers, 2003.

Boyd, Douglas A., *Broadcasting in the Arab World: A Survey of the Electronic Media in the Middle East*, Iowa: Iowa State University Press, 1999.

Dartnell, M., *Insurgency Online: Web Activism and Global Conflict*, Toronto: University of Toronto Press, 2006.

Diamond, E., *The Media Show: The Changing Face of the News, 1985–90*, Cambridge, MA: The MIT Press, 1991.

Dunsky, M., *Pens and Swords: How the American Mainstream Media Report the Israeli–Palestinian Conflict*, Columbia: Columbia University Press, 2008.

Eickelman, Dale F., *New Media in the Muslim World: The Emerging Public Sphere*, Bloomington, IN: Indiana University Press, 2003.

Eldon, Hiebert R., Jean, Gibbons S. and Silver, S., *Exploring Mass Media for a Changing World*, Mahwah, NJ: Lawrence Erlbaum Associates, 2000.

Fackson, Banda, 'Community Broadcasting in Zambia: A Policy Perspective' (unpublished PhD thesis).

Fandy, Mamoun *(Un)civil War of Words: Media and Politics in the Arab World*, Westport, CT and London: Praeger Security International, 2007.

Gerbner, G., Mowlana, H. and Nordenstreng, K., *The Global Media Debate: Its Rise, Fall, and Renewal*, Norwood, NJ: Ablex Publishers, 1993.

Gilboa, Eytan, *Media and Conflict: Framing Issues, Making Policy, Shaping Opinions*, Ardsley, NY: Transnational Publishers, 2002.

Hafez, K., *Mass Media, Politics, and Society in the Middle East*, Cresskill, NJ: Hampton Press, 2001.

Hafez, Kai, 'Guest Editor's Introduction: Mediated Political Communication in the Middle East', *Political Communication* 19 (2), 2002, pp. 121–4.

Hiebert, Ray Eldon and Gibbons, Jean Sheila, *Exploring Mass Media for a Changing World*, Mahwah, NJ: Lawrence Erlbaum Associates, 2000.

Jamal, A., *Media Politics and Democracy in Palestine: Political Culture, Pluralism, and the Palestinian Authority*, Brighton: Sussex Academic Press, 2005.

Jenkins, H. and Thorburn, D., *Democracy and New Media: Media in Transition*, Cambridge, MA: The MIT Press, 2003.

Kamalipour, Y. R., *The U.S. Media and the Middle East: Image and Perception*, Westport, CT: Praeger Publishers, 1997.

Kamalipour, Y. R. and Mowlana, H., *Mass Media in the Middle East: A Comprehensive Handbook*, Westport, CT: Greenwood Press, 1994.

Kamalipour, Y. R. and Snow, N., *War, Media, and Propaganda: A Global Perspective*, Lanham, MD: Rowman & Littlefield Publishers, 2004.

Keeble, Leigh and Loader, Brian D. (eds), *Community Informatics: Shaping Computer-Mediated Social Relations*, London: Routledge, 2001.

Latour, B. and Weibel, P., *Making Things Public: Atmospheres of Democracy*, Cambridge, MA: The MIT Press, 2005.

Levin, T. Y., Frohe, U. and Weibel, P., *CTRL [SPACE]: Rhetorics of Surveillance from Bentham to Big Brother*, Cambridge, MA: The MIT Press, 2002.

Losh, E., *Virtualpolitik: An Electronic History of Government Media-Making in a Time of War, Scandal, Disaster, Miscommunication, and Mistakes*, Cambridge, MA: The MIT Press, 2009.

Lull, J., *Media, Communication, Culture: A Global Approach*, Columbia: Columbia University Press, 2000.

Lynch, M., *Voices of the New Arab Public: Iraq, al-Jazeera, and Middle East Politics Today*, Columbia: Columbia University Press, 2006.

Further Reading

MacArthur, J. R., *Second Front, Censorship and Propaganda in the 1991 Gulf War*, Berkeley, CA: University of California Press, 2004.

McAlister, M., *Epic Encounters: Culture, Media, and US Interests in the Middle East, 1945–2000 (American Crossroads)*, Berkeley, CA: University of California Press, 2005.

Mellor, N., *Modern Arab Journalism: Problems and Prospects*, Edinburgh: Edinburgh University Press, 2008.

Mowlana, H., *Global Communication in Transition: The End of Diversity?*, Thousand Oaks, CA: Sage Publications, 1996.

El-Nawawy, M., Iskandar, A. and Iskandar Farag, A., *Al Jazeera: How the Free Arab News Network Scooped the World and Changed the Middle East*, Boulder, CO: Westview Press, 2002.

Norris, P., Kern, M. and Just, M. R., *Framing Terrorism: The News Media, the Government, and the Public*, New York: Routledge Publishers, 2003.

Al-Obaidi, J. A. and Jawad, A. S., *Media Censorship in the Middle East*, Edwin Mellen Press, 2007.

Pavlik, J. V., *Journalism and New Media*, Columbia: Columbia University Press, 2001.

Pludowski, Tomasz, *How the World's News Media Reacted to 9/11: Essays from around the Globe*, New York: Marquette Books, 2007.

Randall, V., *Democratization and the Media*, London: Frank Cass Publishers, 1998.

Rugh, W. A., *Arab Mass Media: Newspapers, Radio, and Television in Arab Politics*, Westport, CT: Greenwood Publishing Group, 2004.

Sakr, Naomi, *Satellite Realms: Transnational Television, Globalization and the Middle East*, London: I.B. Tauris, 2002.

Sakr, N., *Women and Media in the Middle East: Power through Self-expression*, London: I.B. Tauris, 2004.

SDC/Panos, *Information and Communication Technologies and Large-scale Poverty Reduction Lessons from Asia, Africa, Latin America and the Caribbean*, London: Panos, 2005.

Seib, P., *New Media and the New Middle East*, London: Palgrave Macmillan Publishers, 2007.

Seib, Phillip, *The Al Jazeera Effect: How the New Global Media are Reshaping World Politics*, New York: Potomac Books, 2008.

Semati, M., *Media, Culture and Society in Iran: Living with Globalization and the Islamic State*, New York: Routledge, 2008.

Talbot, M., *Media Discourse: Representation and Interaction*, Edinburgh: Edinburgh University Press, 2007.
Tolson, A., *Media Talk: Spoken Discourse on TV and Radio*, Edinburgh: Edinburgh University Press, 2006.
United Nations Economic Social Commission for Western Asia, *National Profile for the Information Society in Jordan*, ESCWA, 2005.
United Nations Economic Social Commission for Western Asia, *National Profile for the Information Society in the Hashemite Kingdom of Jordan*, ESCWA, 2007.
United Nations Educational, Scientific and Cultural Organization, *Medium Term Strategy for 2008–13*, UNESCO, 2007.
United Nations Millennium Project, *Investing in Development: A Practical Plan to Achieve the Millennium Development Goals*, New York: Earthscan, 2005.
Veer, Peter van der, *Media, War, and Terrorism: Responses from the Middle East and Asia*, New York: RoutledgeCurzon, 2004.
Wolsfeld, Gadi, *Media and the Path to Peace (Community, Society, Politics)*, Cambridge: Cambridge University Press, 2001.
Wolfsfeld, G., *Media and Political Conflict: News from the Middle East*, Cambridge, UK: Cambridge University Press, 1997.
Wolfsfeld, Gadi, *The News Media and Peace Processes: The Middle East and Northern Ireland*, Washington, DC: US Institute of Peace, 2007.
Zayani, M., *The Al Jazeera Phenomenon: Critical Perspectives on New Arab Media*, London: Pluto Press, 2005.

Index

Page numbers in *italics* refer to figures and tables.

101 East (al-Jazeera), 6

A Walk Along the Shore (White), 75
advertising
    revenues, 54, 104, 115, 144–5, 146, 151
    Saudi Arabia's power over, 115, 117
aesthetic values, 76
Afghanistan, war, 2, 4, 58–9, 65
Africa, community radio study, 149
Agaphy (Coptic Orthodox Church channel), 92–3
agency enhancement, 24, 28, 29, 110
AK Party (Turkey), 11–13, 14
America
    Gulf War justification metaphors, 34–5
    image restoration survey, 134
    see also anti-American sentiments; Bush, George W.; United States
Amman Net (Jordan), 143–4, 145, 146, 147, 149–50
Anderson, Jon, 107–8, 124, 125
anti-American sentiments, 57–8, 123, 137
appearances and reality mismatch, 110–11
Arab Human Development Report (2003), 118
Arab–Israeli conflict, 5
Arab League, 112
Arab media charter, 112
Arab public sphere, 103–22
Arab youth and political programming, 110–11
Arabic–French programming, 114
al-Arabiya
    coverage, 126, 135, *135*, 143
    editorial policy, 111, 126, 136, 137
    as a news source, 130–4, *130*, *131*, *132*
Arabs
    accessibility issues, 108, 109–12
    internet implantation, 106
    satellite television imports, 114–15
Aristotle, 76–7
Arnett, Peter, 62
artists, and globalization, 70
Asia, coverage by al-Jazeera, 9, 10, 11
Association Mondiale des Radiodiffuseurs Communautaires (AMARC), 150
Audiovisual Commission (Jordan), 139
axis of evil, 59

Bahrain, GSM technology in, 107
al-Balad *see* Amman Net
Baudrillard, Jean, 63, 112
al-Baz, Osama, 94
BBC (British Broadcasting Corporation)
    Arabic channel, xvi, 3, 125
    and al-Jazeera, 2, 5, 65
    war reports, 62
Beirut Spring, 108–9
Bennett, Lance, 64
Bilder auf Weltreise (Ullrich), 69–70
Bin Laden, Osama, xix, 4
biological weapons, Iraq, 59–60
Blair, Tony, 65
boundaries, crossing, 26–7, 29
Bourdieu, Pierre, 53, 63
bourgeoisie, 21, 104, 105, 108
Brinkerhoff, Jennifer M., 95
British Broadcasting Corporation *see* BBC
Brokaw, Tom, 62
Buckley, Steve, 150
Bush, George W., US President
    addresses and speeches, 39, 58–61, *61*
    al-Jazeera memo, 65
    milestone metaphor, 36–7, 38, 39, 42
    War on Terror, 35, 36, 58
Butrus, Zakariya, 92

Buyukanit, Yasar, 13

Cable News Network *see* CNN
camera phones, censored, 117
cameras, invention, 71, 72
capitalism, 51, 69–70, 76, 104, 105
   global, xvii, xxiii, 111, 116–17, 118
Castells, Manuel, 108, 109
CBS News, 60
censorship, 4, 63–6, 107, 117, 118
Center for Strategic Studies, University of Jordan, 124–5
Central Intelligence Agency (CIA) (US), 57
Chomsky, Noam, 54
Christian–Muslim relations, Egypt, 82, 88–90, 95, 97
Christians, Egyptian, 81–101
CMT (Conceptual Metaphor Theory), 31, 32, 33
CNN (Cable News Network)
   9/11 coverage, 62–3
   Iraq War coverage, 1, 31–45, 62
   rival to al-Jazeera, 2, 4, 5
cognitive linguistics, 32
cognitive metaphor analysis, 36–8
Cohen, Bernard, 53, 63
commercialization, 21, 69–70, 104
commodification, 76, 104, 115, 116
community radio, Jordan, 139, 149–50
Compton, James, 64
computer-aided warfare, 55–6
Conceptual Metaphor Theory (CMT), 31, 32, 33
conversions to Islam, forced, 88–9
Coptic Assembly of America, 93
Coptic Catholic Church, 84
Coptic lobby groups, 86–7
Coptic Orthodox Church, 82, 87, 92, 94, 95–6, 97
Coptic Orthodox community, 83–7
Copts, 81–101
cultural hybridity, xv, 114
Cyprus, 92

Da Vinci, Leonardo, 71
Dahlgren, Peter, 53–4
Daily Mirror, 65
Dasein culture, 70
Dean, Jodi, 109–10
death tolls, Iraq War, 40–1
Debord, Guy, 115

diplomacy, public, 48, 49, 56–8
doctrines of war, 55–6
Doi, Melissa (9/11 victim), 62–3
Doob, Leonard, 52
Dubai, xvi, 117, 126

Egypt
   Arab media charter, 112
   impact of globalization on communal relations, 81–101
   impact on communal relations of new media, 93–6
   internet implantation, 20, 23, 24, 26
   satellite television, 92
Eickelman, Dale, 20, 124, 125
embedded journalists, 2, 64
emigration, Middle Eastern Christians, 85
English-Lueck, Jan, 27
Enlightenment, European, 71
Entman, Robert, 6
Erdogan, Recep Tayyip (Turkish PM), 12, 15
ESN (Egypt), 106

Fabiszak, Malgorzata, 31
Facebook, xv, 119
'Facing West from California's Shores' (Whitman), 75–6
Fandy, Mamoun, 111, 143
Fann FM (Jordan), 145
Farah al Nas FM (Jordan), 150
film, 72–3, 78
foreign policy
   American, 49, 53, 57
   Qatari, 3, 111
   Saudi Arabian, 111
Foucault, Michel, 110
Fraser, Nancy, 108
freedom, editorial, 3–4, 19–30, 50, 64–5
French–Arabic programming, 114
Frost, David, 5, 6
Frost Over The World (al-Jazeera), 6

Gamson, William A., 58
Gandhi, M. K., 47
Gaza, Israeli attack, 125–6
geocultural regions, 3
Germany, wartime propaganda, 52
Ghareeb, Edmund, 91
al Ghraib prison, 63
Giddens, Antony, 55, 56
Gitlin, Todd, 58

INDEX

global convergence, 114
globalization, xvii, xx, 26, 57
   and image culture, 69–70, 77–8
   impact on communal relations in Egypt, 81–101
Goebbels, Paul Joseph, 52
governmentality, Foucault's concept of, 110
Gramsci, Antonio, 53
   see also hegemony
Grimes, John, 116
GSM technology, xviii, 107
Guardian, 14
Gul, Abdullah, 13, 14
Gulf Cooperation Council (GCC), 140
Gulf War, 1, 34–5, 55, 62

Habermas, Jürgen, 50–1, 104, 108, 119
   see also public spheres
hacking, of al-Jazeera, 4
Hamad, Emir of Qatar, 3, 65, 115, 125
Hamas, suicide bombers, 11
Harris Interactive Jordan Media Survey, 139, 144, 148
headscarves, in Turkey, 14–15
Hear, Nicholas van, 83
hegemony, 53, 69, 77, 108, 116, 118
   counter-hegemony, 3, 117
Heikal, Muhammed Hassanein, 5
Herman, Edward, 54
horizontal network society, 108
al-Hurra channel, xix, 127, 136
Hussein, Saddam, 35, 36, 59–60
al-Hyat channel (Cyprus), 92

al-Ibrahim, Walid, 126
ICT *see* information communications technology
idealism–realism debate, 76–7
image and reality, 112–13
image culture, 69–79
industrialization, of war, 55
Information and Decision Support Center (IDSC) (Egypt), 24
information communications technology (ICT)
   Arab public sphere, 103–22
   media-based Arab, 105–9
   religious diaspora in Egypt, 81–101
Information Operations (IO), 55
information warfare, 55–6
International Religious Freedom Act, 94, 95

internet
   cafes, 24
   institutional implantation, 21, 23, 24, 25, 26
   origins, 21
   radio, 143–4, 147
Iran, and axis of evil, 59
Iraq, 4, 59, 59–60, 106
   see also Gulf War
Iraq War
   CNN and al-Jazeera discourse, 31–45
   embedded journalists, 2
Iraqi Governing Council, 4
Irbid (Jordan), 150
Islam, conversions to, 88–9
Islamic Action Front (Jordan), 134, 137
Islamic fundamentalism, 1–2
Islamists, Turkish, 12, 13, 14

Japan, wartime radio propaganda, 52
al-Jazeera, 41, 106, 115, 135–6
   alleged bombing by US, 4, 64–5
   Asia coverage, 9, 10, 11
   criticism of coverage, 4, 143
   editorial policy, 4–6, 111, 125–6, 136, 137
   Iraq War coverage, 31–45
   language, 9–11, *10*, *11*, 113–14
   as a news source, 4, 6–9, *7*, *8*, *9*, 130–4, *130*, *131*, *132*
   political coverage, 3–4, 5, 11–15, 135, *135*
   prime-time broadcasting, 1–18
   website, 36–8
al-Jazeera International, 5, 13, 32
Johnson, Mark, 31, 32
Jordan
   internet implantation, 20, 23, 24, 26, 124, *129*
   local radio, 139–53, *157*
   news sources, *127*, 128, *128*, 132–3, 134–6
   satellite television, 124–37, *124*, *127*
Jordanian Fund for Human Resources and Development (JOHUD), 150
Jordanian National Television (JTV), 126, 130–4, *130*, *131*, *132*, *135*, 136
journalism, credibility and control, 49–50
journalists, role of, 50, 63–6
justification of war, 48, 56–7, 58–60

Karam, Imad, 110
al-*Keraza* (magazine), 96
Kernall, Samuel, 58
Khan, Riz, 5, 6

[165]

Khatib, Lina, 108–9
kidnapping, of Coptic girls, 88–9
Kurds, and satellite television, 91
al-Kush (Egypt), violence, 89–90
Kuttab, David, 143
Kuwait, xvi, xvii, 34–5, 125
  see also Gulf War

Lakoff, George, 31, 32, 34–5
language issues, 11, 12, 31, 113–14, 126
Lawrence of Arabia (Thomas Edward Lawrence), 73–4
League of Arab States (LAS), 140
Lefebvre, Henri, 116
Leonard, Mark, 57–8
Lib (Jordan), e-village project, 149
Libya, GSM technology, 107
linguistics, cognitive, 32
Lippmann, Walter, 50, 66
lobbying, on Coptic émigrée sites, 87–90, 95–6, 97
Lule, Jack, 35–6
Lynch, Marc, 109, 113

Mandaville, Peter G., 82
manufacture of consent, 66
Manufacturing Consent (Herman and Chomsky), 54
mapping, metaphors, 33–4, 35
Marqus, Bishop, 94
Marxism, 116
Mattelart, Armand, 56, 57
McCombs, Maxwell, 53
McQuail, Denis, 53
MED TV (Turkey), 91
media, and power, 69–79
media bias, 136, 137
Mellor, Noha, 108, 114
Melody radio station (Jordan), 144
metaphors
  conceptual, 32–4
  milestone, 32, 33–4, 36–41, 42–4
  of war, 34–6, 42–3
Metaphors We Live By (Lakoff and Johnson), 31, 32
Meunier, Michael, 90
Middle East
  Christians in, 85, 90, 92
  internet implantation, 19–30, *22*
  satellite television, 2, 3, 9, 10, 123
milestone, metaphor, 32, 33–4, 36–41, 42–4

Millennium Development Goals (MDGs), United Nations, 139, 140
Millennium Summit, New York (2005), 140
Mleih (Jordan), e-village project, 149
mobile telephones, 107, 147
Modigliani, André, 58
Montagu, Lady Mary Wortley, 72
moral justification, for Gulf War, 34
movement/journey scenario, Iraq War, 36–8
moving images, 72–3, 78
Mubarak, Hosni, President of Egypt, 94
Musa (Coptic Orthodox Bishop of Youth), 92
Muslim
  world, *22*
Muslim Brotherhood (Jordan), 134, 137
Muslim–Christian relations, Egypt, 82, 88–90, 95, 97
Muslim world, 21, *22*, 29, 123

Nasser, Gamal Abdel, President of Egypt, 85
nation-as-family metaphor, 33
National Profile for the Information Society in Jordan (ESCWA), 141–2
National Security Act (1947) (US), 56–7
National Security Council (US), 57
Nazi propaganda, 52
NBC News, 35–6, 62
Neo-Marxists, 53
Netherlands, The, 69–70
network-centric operations (NCO), 55–6
network-centric warfare (NCW), 55–6
neutrality, of media, 63–4, 119
New Media in the Muslim World (Eikelman and Anderson), 20
New World Order/Disorder, 1, 2
New York Times, 4, 60
newsreels, German, 52
Nietzsche, Friedrich, 70–1
Nilesat satellite, 92
Nimri, Eman, 150
9/11 attacks, 2, 35, 60
  aftermath, 57–8, 60–1, *61*
  media coverage, 48, 62–3, 125
North Korea, and axis of evil, 59
Norton, Augustus Richard, 81

Obama, Barack, US President, xix, 134
Office of the Press Secretary (US), 64
Operation Enduring Freedom (Afghanistan), 58–9
Operation Iraqi Freedom, 58

opinion polls, 60
Opposite Direction, The (al-Jazeera), 4–5

Padania, Sameer, 140, 149, 151
Palestine, 143
Palestinians, 5, 126
Patriarch of Alexandria and all Africa, 84
patriotism, and Iraq War coverage, 63
patronage, 23, 24, 26, 27
Patterson, Thomas, 63
Pennsylvania, University of, 55
Pentagon (US), 55, 60
People and Power (al-Jazeera), 5–6
Peri, Yoram, 64
Petit Prince, Le (Saint-Exupéry), 74
photography, 72, 73
Plato, 76–7
political programming, and Arab youth, 110–11
politics, international, role of mass media, 1–2, 3
pornography, 117
postmodernism, 75, 76
poverty survey, Jordan, 132–3
Powell, Colin, 65
power, and the media, 69–79
private ownership
  radio, in Jordan, 143–7, 151, *155*
  satellite television, 115
private sector investment, 140, 146
progress-oriented scenario, 39
propaganda, 51, 52–4, 57, 60–1, *61*
Protestants, in Egypt, 84
psychological warfare, 56, 58
public diplomacy, 48, *49*, 56–8
Public Opinion (Lippmann), 50
public opinion, impact of Arab satellite channels, 123–37
public sector, internet implantation, 25, 26
public spheres, 48, 104–5, 108–9
  Arab, 109–12, 123
  as spectacle, 112–19
  see also Habermas
public, the new, 107–8

al-Qaeda, 1–2, 125
al-Qaradawi, Yousef, 5
Qatar, 3–4, 5, 107, 111, 114, 125
Queen Zein Al-Sharaf Institute (Jordan), 150
Quran FM (Jordan), 145

Qur'an, radio coverage in Jordan, 146

radio
  in Jordan, 139–53, *157*
  use by President Bush, 60–1
  and wartime propaganda, 52
rape metaphor, 34, 35
Raphael, 76–7
realism–idealism debate, 76–7
reality, created by media, 112
refugees, internet usage by, 24
Religion and Life (al-Jazeera), 5
religious diaspora, 81–101
Renaissance, European, 70, 71
reporters, war, 64
Reporters Without Borders, 65
Republican People's Party (RPP) (Turkey), 14, 15
rescue scenario, Gulf War, 34, 35
Riz Khan Show, The (al-Jazeera), 6
Robertson, Roland, 83
Rotana radio station (Jordan), 144
Rowe, Paul S., 95
Royal Scientific Society (RSS) (Jordan), 24

El Sadat, Anwar, President of Egypt, 85
Saint-Exupéry, Antoine de, 74
Sakr, Naomi, 3, 91, 111
satellite television
  Arab, 106, 110, 113–14, 123–37
  ownership, 111
  use by Copts, 91–3
Saudi Arabia
  advertising power, 115
  Arab media charter, 112
  internet implantation, 20, 23, 24–5, 26
  satellite television, 106, 111
  ulema, 117
Sawt al-Ghad radio station (Jordan), 144, 146
Sawt al-Madinah radio station (Jordan), 143
Scholte, Jan Aart, 82
School of Athens, The (Raphael), 76–7
search engines, 116
Second World War, radio propaganda, 52
secular protests, Turkey, 12, 13, 14
self-defence scenario, Gulf War, 34, 35
September 11, 2001 *see* 9/11 attacks
Sezer, Ahmet Necdet, 13
Shaw, Donald, 53
Shenouda III, Patriarch, 84, 87, 90, 95–6

short-wave radio propaganda, Second World War, 52
Silicon Valley (USA), 27–8
Silvani, Francesca, 140, 149, 151
Simulations (Baudrillard), 112
Situationist International, 115
social welfare, 105
spin, 60–1
state accountability, 104–5
state control, 3, 53, 57, 58, 106, 107
Strukturwandel der Öffenlicheit (Habermas), 104
subaltern counter publics, 108
Sudan, and GSM technology, 107
suffering, trivialisation of, 47
surveillance, 56, 57
Syria, internet implantation, 20, 23, 24, 26
Syrian Computer Society (SCS), 24, 26, 27

telemedicine, 23, 24–5
television wars, 62–3
Thomson, Charles, 52
Thus Spoke Zarathustra (Nietzsche), 70
total war, 56
trivialisation, 47, 62
truth, search for, 71–2, 76–7, 77–8
Tunisia, internet governance, 117
Turkey, presidential election, 11–15

ulema, xiv, 117
Ullrich, Wolfgang, 69–70
United Arab Emirate (UAE), 106, 107
United Nations
 Development Fund for Women (UNIFEM), 149
 Economic Social Commission for Western Asia (ESCWA), 141–2
 Educational, Scientific and Cultural Organization (UNESCO), 139, 149
 Millennium Development Goals, 139, 140
United States
 Copts in, 88, 90, 93, 94
 doctrines and policies, 53–4, 55–6, 56–7
 grants and aid, 86, 94, 150
 New World Order/Disorder, 1, 2
 propaganda, Second World War, 52
 satellite television, 4, 114
 US Congress International Religious Freedom Act (1998), 86
 as victim, 35
 see also America; anti-American sentiments; Bush, George W.

verbal culture, 79
violence
 American media and, 53–4
 control, 55
 against Copts, 84, 88, 89–90
vision, selectivity of, 74–5

Wafd Party (Egypt), 84
(al) Wakeel, Mohammed, 145–6
War is Business metaphor, 34
War is Politics metaphor, 34
War on Terror, 31, 35, 47–67, 49
Warf, Barney, 116
Washington Post, 60
al-Watan radio station (Jordan), 146, 147
Watani (newspaper), 95
Weapons of Mass Destruction (WMDs), 35, 59–60
Webster, Frank, 55
West, programming imported from, 114–15
White, Kenneth, 75
Whitman, Walt, 75–6
Who Wants to Be a Millionaire?, 114, 115
Williams, Raymond, 53
Wissa (Coptic Orthodox bishop), 90
With Heikal (al-Jazeera), 5
World Assembly of Community Radio Broadcasters Conference (2006), 150
World Summit on the Information Society (WSIS), Tunisia (2005), 117, 118

Yarmouk FM (Jordan), 150
Yemen, 106, 107
youth development, 140–1, 148
YouTube, 119

Zarqa (Jordan), 150

Stafford Library
Columbia College
1001 Rogers Street
Columbia, Missouri 65216